FISHES
OF THE
OKAVANGO DELTA
& CHOBE RIVER, BOTSWANA

Mike Bruton, Glenn Merron & Paul Skelton

T0353015

Mike Bruton
Honorary Research Associate, South African Institute for
Aquatic Biodiversity, Grahamstown, South Africa

Glenn Merron
President, Inland Ecosystems, Reno, Nevada, USA

Paul Skelton
Honorary Research Associate, South African Institute for Aquatic Biodiversity,
Grahamstown, South Africa and Science Director,
Wild Bird Trust – National Geographic Okavango Wilderness Project

Published by Struik Nature
   (an imprint of Penguin Random House
   South Africa (Pty) Ltd)
Reg. No. 1953/000441/07
The Estuaries No. 4, Oxbow Crescent
   Century City, 7441 South Africa
PO Box 1144, Cape Town,
   8000 South Africa

First published in 2018 by Struik Nature

10 9 8 7 6 5 4 3 2 1

Publisher: Pippa Parker
Managing editor: Helen de Villiers
Editor: Emily Donaldson
Designers: Gillian Black, Dominic Robson
Cartographer: Liezel Bohdanowicz
Proofreader: Thea Grobbelaar
Artists: Liz Tarr (EMT) and Dave Voorvelt (DV)

Reproduction by Resolution Colour (Pty) Ltd
Printed and bound in China

Print: 9781775845058
E-pub: 9781775845065

FSC
MIX
Paper from
responsible sources
www.fsc.org   FSC® C101537

Visit **www.penguinrandomhouse.co.za**
and join the Struik Nature Club for updates,
news, events and special offers.

ACKNOWLEDGMENTS

Our research in the Okavango Delta was carried out while we were staff members of the JLB Smith Institute of Ichthyology (now the South African Institute for Aquatic Biodiversity, SAIAB) in Grahamstown. We are grateful to the Botswana Department of Agriculture: Fisheries Unit for permission to do this research. Financial support for our research was provided by the Okavango Wildlife Society, Kalahari Conservation Society, World Wildlife Fund, Rhodes University and the JLB Smith Institute of Ichthyology. We are also extremely grateful to Steve Boyes and John Hilton of 'The Wild Bird Trust – National Geographic Okavango Wilderness Project' for their generous financial support of this book.

We thank the following colleagues for assistance during fieldwork: Pete Smith, Jeff Bowles, Ted Baines, Humphry Greenwood, P.J. Bestelink, Shirley Bethune, Tom Hecht, Rex Quick, John Rogers, Pete White, James Molefne and Vuyisile Yose. Ben van der Waal, Roger Bills and Denis Tweddle have worked closely with Paul Skelton in the Namibian reaches of the region over many years, which has led to a better understanding of this dynamic system.

We are grateful to Angus Paterson, MD of SAIAB, for permission to use colour illustrations of fishes from the Institute's archives, and to Sally Schramm, Maditaba Meltaf and Penny Haworth for their valuable assistance. We are also grateful to Kabelo Senyatso, President of BirdLife Botswana, and Map Ives, National Rhino Coordinator of Botswana, for assistance with the Setswana names of fishes. We also thank Pippa Parker, Helen de Villiers, Emily Donaldson, Gillian Black and Dominic Robson of Struik Nature for the professional way in which they have guided this book through the production process.

CONTENTS

SPONSOR'S FOREWORD

The waters of the Okavango Delta do not all fall from the sky or rise up from the Kalahari Desert. These life-giving floodwaters come from two distant rivers, the Cubango and Cuito, which originate in the central Angolan highlands.

In 2015 the National Geographic Okavango Wilderness Project (NGOWP) was established to explore these and other little-known rivers that feed the delta in an effort to protect these vital sources of fresh water. Professor Paul Skelton, one of the contributing authors to this book, joined our team as chief scientist and lead ichthyologist.

Our first expedition, the 'Source to Sand Megatransect' pioneered access to the unexplored source lake of the Cuito. It was a dream to sample the poorly known waters of this remote and pristine 1,8 km-long lake, which is surrounded by previously unknown stratified peat deposits and unending miombo woodland. Each morning we were all captivated by the overnight catch: the diminutive and sometimes colourful topminnows, barbs, mormyrids, climbing perch, grunters, bream and many others told the story of these dynamic, living rivers. A climbing perch caught at the source was thought to be either a new species or a known species previously recorded only from the Congo Basin, while the first Zambezi grunter caught just below the source lake demonstrated a distant connection to the Zambezi River. These stories span millions of years.

Studies are ongoing and, to date, the project has revealed at least 24 new species of plants and animals and 38 species new to Angola, along with countless species range extensions. It is likely that these figures will increase, with new species yet to be discovered.

We are proud sponsors of this publication by Mike Bruton, Glenn Merron and Paul Skelton, and we recognize Paul, in particular, for his work with our team and his commitment to the preservation of the delta and the rivers that sustain it. The future of the fish species profiled in this book will not be secure until we protect the headwaters of the Okavango River Basin in Angola, and mitigate the potential impacts of dams, disease, invasive species and fish farming upstream in Angola and Namibia.

We hope that in a hundred years visitors to the Okavango Delta will still be able to look into the crystal-clear waters and use this book to identify the diversity of fish species that live in this unique wetland wilderness, an oasis in the desert and a sanctuary for biodiversity.

Dr Steve Boyes
Founding Trustee, The Wild Bird Trust
Founder, National Geographic Okavango Wilderness Project
Fellow, National Geographic Society

AUTHORS' PREFACE

This book is an introduction to the fishes of the Okavango Delta, Botswana, which have been the subject of intensive study by scientists from the South African Institute for Aquatic Biodiversity (SAIAB, previously the JLB Smith Institute of Ichthyology) in Grahamstown, South Africa. This research initially covered the taxonomy, diversity, distribution, ecology and behaviour of Okavango fishes but was extended, in collaboration with the Botswana authorities, to include fisheries management and the impact of tsetse fly spraying on the fish.

Our research was initiated in 1979 and continued intensively until 1992. Thereafter Paul Skelton and Roger Bills undertook further work in the Okavango as part of Conservation International's Rapid Bioassessment Programme until 1999. The Okavango expeditions included scientists from the JLB Smith Institute of Ichthyology as well as from the Department of Ichthyology & Fisheries Science, Rhodes University, University of Botswana, Natural History Museum (England), University of KwaZulu-Natal, University of Guelph (Canada), University of Tel Aviv (Israel) and others.

During the research programme temporary field stations were established adjacent to the Thamalakane River near Crocodile Camp (courtesy of De Beers and the Kalahari Conservation Society) as well as at Seronga, Nxaragha Lagoon, Maqwexana Pools in Moremi Game Reserve and Shakawe. Fish specimens collected during the fieldwork were deposited in the collection of the JLB Smith Institute of Ichthyology (now SAIAB) in Grahamstown, with representative samples donated to the Botswana National Museum in Gaborone.

The research team was led by Mike Bruton, then Director of the JLB Smith Institute of Ichthyology, with an increasingly important role being played by Paul Skelton, initially through the Albany Museum and then through SAIAB. He continues to be involved in research on the fishes of the Okavango system through the National Geographic Okavango Wilderness Project. Glenn Merron from the University of Michigan led the field research from 1983 and set the stage for other students to pursue in-depth studies there.

We have also included information on the fishes of the Chobe River on the northern border of Botswana, even though it is part of a different river system (upper Zambezi), in order to cover all the fishes of northern Botswana. Botswana also has rivers along its southern and eastern borders (Orange and Limpopo systems respectively) that provide habitat for additional fish species, but they are not mentioned here.

THE OKAVANGO DELTA AND CHOBE RIVER

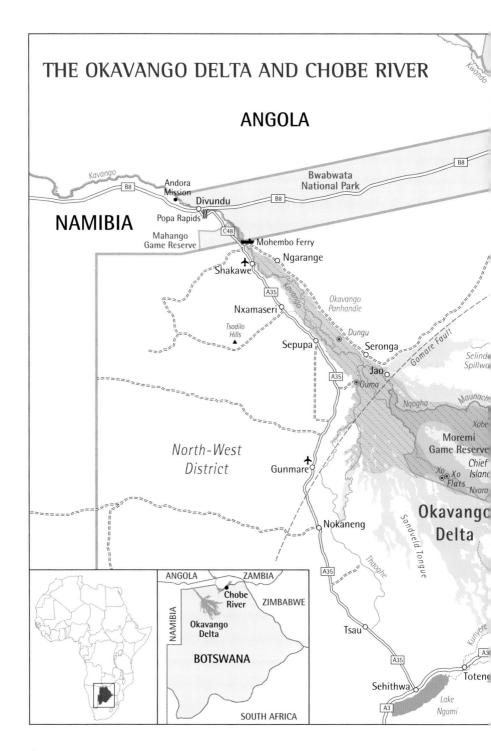

ANGOLA

Kwando

Kavango

B8

Andora
Mission

Divundu

B8

Bwabwata
National Park

B8

NAMIBIA

Popa Rapids

Mahango
Game Reserve

C48

Mohembo Ferry

Ngarange

Shakawe

A35

Kavango

Okavango
Panhandle

Nxamaseri

Tsodilo
Hills

Dungu

Sepupa

Seronga

Gomare Fault

A35

Jao

Guma

Selinda
Spillway

Ngogha

Maunach

North-West
District

Gunmare

Xobe

Moremi
Game Reserve

Chief
Island

Xo Xo
Flats

Nxara

Nokaneng

Sandveld Tongue

Okavango
Delta

Thaoghe

A35

ANGOLA

ZAMBIA

Chobe
River

ZIMBABWE

NAMIBIA

Okavango
Delta

Tsau

Kunyere

BOTSWANA

A3

A35

Totene

Sehithwa

A3

SOUTH AFRICA

Lake
Ngami

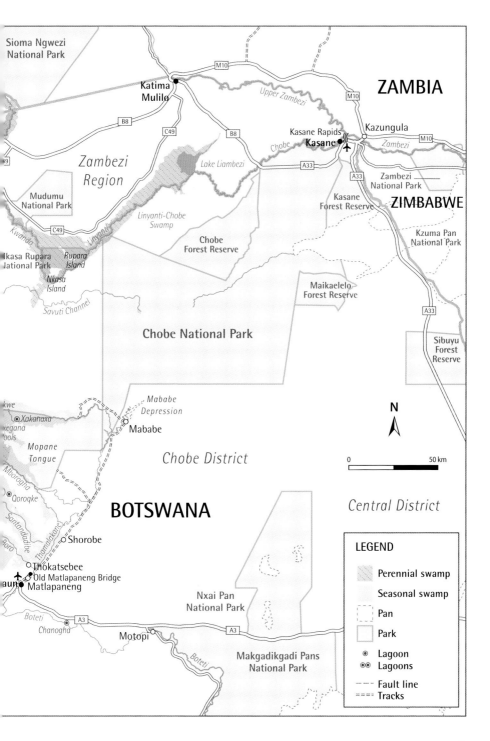

Sioma Ngwezi
National Park

Katima
Mulilo

ZAMBIA

Upper Zambezi

M10

M10

B8

C49

B8

Kasane Rapids
Chobe Kasane

Kazungula

M10

Zambezi

*Zambezi
Region*

Lake Liambezi

A33

A33

Zambezi
National Park

Mudumu
National Park

Kasane
Forest Reserve

ZIMBABWE

Linyanti-Chobe
Swamp

C49

Kwando

Linyanti

Kzuma Pan
National Park

Ikasa Rupara
Iational Park

*Rupara
Island*

Chobe
Forest Reserve

Nkasa
Island

Maikaelelo
Forest Reserve

Savuti Channel

Chobe National Park

A33

Sibuyu
Forest
Reserve

kwe

Xakanaxa

xegana
ools

*Mababe
Depression*

Mababe

N

Mopane
Tongue

Chobe District

0   50 km

Mborogha

Qoroqke

Santandadibe

Boro

Thamalakane

BOTSWANA

Central District

Shorobe

LEGEND

Thokatsebee
Old Matlapaneng Bridge
aun Matlapaneng

Nxai Pan
National Park

Boteti

A3

Chanogha

Motopi

A3

Boteti

Makgadikgadi Pans
National Park

Perennial swamp

Seasonal swamp

Pan

Park

Lagoon
Lagoons

Fault line
Tracks

INTRODUCTION

An estimated 11,000 million cubic metres of water flows into the Okavango Delta annually. This is augmented by a further 5,000 million cubic metres of local rainfall. Although over 90% of this water eventually evaporates in the desert, it is the lifeblood of the Okavango Delta, one of the most interesting and valuable wetlands in the world.

With just 87 fish species, the Okavango Delta and Chobe River may not boast the diversity of some other African freshwater ecosystems, but they do have a very high diversity of families (15) and especially genera (39), particularly when compared with the African Great Lakes, which are dominated by one family (the cichlids) and just a few genera.

This diversity is partly a consequence of the varied origins of the fishes: no fewer than 60 species recorded here are of tropical origin and reach their southern limit of distribution in the Okavango Delta or lower Kavango River. An additional 21 species extend further southwards, along the warm Mozambique Plain on the east coast, and into northern Zululand, while six species are distributed widely in southern Africa and extend northwards into the Chobe River, Okavango Delta and beyond. Thus, the Okavango Delta, Zambezi system and coastal rivers of southeast Africa comprise an important transitional zone between the tropical faunas to the north and the subtropical and subtemperate faunas to the south.

The other key factor influencing the diversity of families and genera is the varied ecology and habitats provided by the Okavango Delta and Chobe River.

The fish fauna of the two systems comprises:
- minnows, yellowfishes and labeos (21 species, 24.1% of the total),
- catfishes (20 species, 23%),
- cichlids (river breams, sargos, largemouth breams, halplochromines and tilapiines; 19 species, 21.8%) and
- snoutfishes (11 species, 12.6%).

The catfishes include four mountain catfish species and sand catlets, six air-breathing catfishes, one claroteid catfish, eight squeakers and suckermouths, and one silver catfish.

Structure and ecology of the Okavango Delta

The same geological processes that created the lakes and swamps of Africa's Great Rift Valley also produced the Okavango Delta, located at the valley's southern end. In the distant past the Kavango River flowed into the Indian Ocean, probably through the Limpopo River. The course of the lower Kavango River was later interrupted by the

Opposite: Satellite image of the Okavango Delta, showing the panhandle and the fan-like shape (NASA)

Permanent lagoon habitat in the lower Kavango River

movement of tectonic plates, resulting in the formation of a vast inland delta. Such a delta does not reach the sea; instead, its waters evaporate or dissipate into the ground, as is the case for the Okavango Delta.

The Kavango River originates in the highlands of Angola, where it is known as the Cubango, and travels for over 1,000 km before entering Botswana at Mohembo. The annual flood reaches Mohembo in February/March each year.

The delta slopes very gently from north to south, with a gradient of about one metre in four kilometres. It is so flat that termite mounds are often the highest landforms, and copses of trees and eventually islands surrounded by floodwaters may form around them. There are very few surface rocks or stones in the delta: the entire Kalahari Basin is filled with windblown sand underlain, often at considerable depths, by volcanic or sedimentary rocks. The area is tectonically active, and the whole basin is therefore prone to earthquakes. (The last major quake in the Okavango Delta, in 1952, measured 6.7 on the Richter Scale, which is at the upper end of a 'strong' earthquake.)

Narrow channel habitat in the perennial swamp

Channel habitat in the riverine panhandle

Perennial swamp habitat

Regions of the Okavango Delta

The delta comprises three distinct regions – the riverine panhandle, the perennial swamp and the seasonal swamp.

The riverine panhandle
The 'panhandle', so called because it resembles the handle of a frying pan, is a channel through which the Kavango River flows from Shakawe to south of Seronga in a 15-km-wide corridor between two geological fault lines. The river meanders through papyrus-filled swampland, between banks of compacted sand and peat, and south of the village of Seronga crosses the Gomare Fault where it enters the perennial swamp.

The perennial swamp
At the northern end of the perennial swamp the river splits into three main channels:
• the Nqogha-Maunachira-Mborogha-Santandadibe system that drains to the east,
• the Xo-Boro system that drains to the southeast, and
• the Thaoghe system that drains southwards along the western edge of the delta.
    The upper reaches of these three systems are permanently flooded, as are the floodplains that lie adjacent to the first two systems for most of their length. The third

Floating water chestnut *Trapa natans* is typical of both the perennial and seasonal swamps.

Water lilies are common in permanent waterbodies in the perennial and seasonal swamps.

system, the Thaoghe River, began choking up with plants about 120 years ago and now has a very limited flow.

The perennial swamp covers an area of about 6,000 km² and is characterized by groves of wild date palm *(Phoenix reclinata)*, vast beds of papyrus, islands rimmed with trees, and lagoons covered with water lilies.

Within the perennial swamp there are oxbow lakes, waterbodies that form when the river cuts across a wide meander to form an isolated, crescent-shaped lake that also has some features of a river. The perennial swamp is a relatively stable and predictable environment and supports a diverse population of fish species, some of which are not found in the seasonal swamp.

The seasonal swamp

The seasonal swamp, which is flooded between May and September each year, covers an area of over 12,000 km², and is fed by water flowing down river channels from the perennial swamp, as well as by water flowing across the floodplains. These floodwaters move slowly through the network of channels and floodplains, taking around four months to cover the distance of about 250 km from Mohembo (approximately 1,000 m above sea level) to Maun (935 m).

Although the seasonal swamp is a highly changeable habitat depending on flood conditions, its ecology is relatively predictable due to the reliability of the annual floods. The southeasterly drainage channels in the seasonal swamp eventually empty into the Thamalakane River, which runs in a southwesterly direction. During high floods this water flows into the Nghabe River and eventually reaches Lake Ngami. The main inflow into Lake Ngami is, however, from the Kunyere River via Toteng.

During the annual flood the seasonal swamp develops into a vast floodplain covered by expansive stands of sawgrass (a tall sedge with serrated leaves) and *Phragmites* reeds, with sparse stands of papyrus. Within the floodplains there are:

- *oshanas*, small channels leading from a river through its floodplain, and
- *madibas*, lagoons or small, permanent lakes.

Typical seasonal swamp habitat

Shallow vlei habitat in the seasonal swamp

LAKES NGAMI AND LIAMBEZI

Lake Ngami is a closed drainage system ('endorheic' lake) with no outflow, and its water level fluctuates widely depending on inflow. In the 19th century it had an area of over 200 km² but, over the past century, it has dried up occasionally, most recently in 1982. Today it receives a steady annual inflow of water and is an impressive lake that attracts birders and other tourists bringing much needed revenue to the communities of Toteng, Sehithwa and elsewhere. It is also subject to intensive semi-commercial fishing.

At one stage it seemed that Lake Ngami was destined to end up like the Mababe Depression, which was once a lake fed by the Savuti Channel but is now dry grassland. However, good water management by Botswana's authorities has ensured that it receives a steady inflow and is now a permanent lake.

Lake Liambezi, between the Linyanti and Chobe rivers in the Zambezi Region of Namibia, has been less fortunate, as its water flow has reduced substantially in recent years and it has been more or less dry since 1985, although it did have some water between 2002 and 2017. This once productive lake is a shadow of its former self and provides a clear indication of what can happen to a wetland if its water inflow is reduced.

In the Chobe and upper Zambezi floodplains there are also *dambos*, drainage lines in areas of impeded drainage. Clayey soils cause waterlogging and the exclusion of trees. *Dambos* are typically found in miombo woodlands, which are seasonal tropical woodland, savanna and dry forest biomes that are widespread in south-central Africa and are characterized by miombo *(Brachystegia)* trees.

When water levels recede the floodplain is reduced to:

- *mulapos*, temporary waterbodies in small depressions or drainage lines, and
- vleis, shallow marshes with emergent plants.

Some *mulapos*, when they dry out, leave a white crust or *trona* on their surface. This comprises dried salts, mainly sodium bicarbonate, from the groundwater.

Within the perennial and seasonal swamps there are numerous islands, the largest of which is Chief's Island, which was created by tectonic uplift. Smaller islands are formed around termite mounds or from ground that has been elevated due to channel blockages. Islands increase the diversity of habitats by breaking up the extensive swamp and providing transition zones (ecotones) between wet and dry land.

The Okavango Delta therefore comprises three distinct but interlinked wetland systems with widely fluctuating, yet predictable, ecological conditions, depending on the state and size of the annual flood. This results in a wide variety of habitats and ecotones in which fish species and other aquatic animals (and plants) can live and thrive.

The breeding, feeding and migration cycles of most Okavango and Chobe fishes are dictated by the annual patterns of flooding and draining of the floodplains, *madibas, mulapos*, vleis and marshes.

Aquatic habitats in the Okavango Delta and Chobe River

Nine main habitat types occur in the Okavango Delta and Chobe River areas:

- **Main river channels:** The main river flowing into the Okavango Delta is the Kavango River from Namibia. In the Okavango/Zambezi regions all the waterways have the potential to be connected. The open-water river channels are deep and slow-flowing and contained within permanent sandy banks. Their substrates comprise scoured sand with little detritus. They have few or no floating plants and provide midwater (pelagic) habitats for strong-swimming fish species. Some river reaches have steep, or gradually sloping, sandy river banks that offer shallow but exposed habitats for small species or for the juveniles of large species.
- **Rapids and riffles:** This habitat is rare in the area, but rocky rapids do occur at Popa Rapids on the Kavango River in Namibia and at the Kasane Rapids on the Chobe River near Kasane.
- **Side channels:** Side channel habitats are narrower than main river channels and are lined with emergent plants, especially papyrus *(Cyperus papyrus)*, common reed *(Phragmites australis)* and miscanthus grass *(Miscanthus junceus)*. Their substrates comprise mainly sand, although detritus does accumulate along the fringes under the stems of emergent plants, which provide a diverse environment.
- **Lagoons *(madibas):*** These small, permanent lakes are scattered throughout the perennial swamp, with a few in the seasonal swamp, and typically occur where channels merge or oxbow lakes have been formed. They comprise still midwater habitats and diverse fringe habitats with abundant emergent and floating plants. Their substrates are muddy and covered with detritus. Hippos, Cape clawless otters, Nile crocodiles, Okavango hinged terrapins, and various snakes and frogs

P Levey/Flickr

Kasane Rapids on the Chobe River near Kasane

M. Bruton

Purple heron eating a snake catfish, Chobe River floodplain

P Skelton

Guma Lagoon, a *madiba* or permanent lagoon

are common in open water, or along its fringes, as well as in swamp habitats in the Okavango and Chobe areas. Hippos play a particularly important ecological role, as they fertilize waterbodies with their copious dung and also create and maintain open channels in dense swamps. African jacanas are common on the floating lily beds, and Pel's fishing owl, which feeds almost exclusively on fish, is found in quiet inlets with overhanging trees.

- **Perennial swamps:** These permanently inundated wetlands are found along the edge of the riverine panhandle and in the northern perennial swamp and Linyanti-Chobe Swamp, and are also formed after the flood reaches the southern seasonal swamp. They are dominated by floating-leaved, submerged and emergent plants and have substrates that vary from sand to silt and peat beds. The floating-leaved plants, which include day water lily *(Nymphaea nouchali)* and water chestnut *(Trapa natans)*, provide shelter from aerial predators, such as fish eagles, fishing owls and kingfishers, and also from predators stalking along the water's edge, such as herons, egrets and storks.

A giraffe grazes in dry seasonal floodplain habitat.   Elephants on the floodplain of the Chobe River

Diverse underwater habitats and nurseries are created by the dominant submerged plants, particuluarly water lettuce *(Ottelia ulvifolia)* and by emergent plants, especially papyrus, common reeds, miscanthus grass and bulrushes *(Typha capensis)*.

- **Seasonal floodplains:** The seasonally inundated floodplains in the southern delta are a quite different type of habitat from the perennial swamp. Unlike the perennial swamp, where the water levels remain high and more or less constant, water levels in the seasonal swamp vary widely from dry to shallow, with the level of flooding also varying widely from year to year. When the floodwaters arrive in winter, the grass cover (mainly *Panicum* and *Cymbopogon* species and *Cynodon dactylon*) is submerged and water lilies and other plants invade the wetland, which has a silty or peaty substrate and provides a diverse, though temporary, habitat for small fish. In spring and early summer the floodwaters recede, and the seasonal swamp reverts to grassland, which is then inhabited by herds of elephant, buffalo, lechwe, tsessebe, blue wildebeest and Burchell's zebra, which feed and then deposit their droppings,

Dried ephemeral pan adjacent to the Chobe River

Marsh habitat on the fringe of the perennial swamp

thus supplying natural fertilizer for the next flood cycle. Large numbers of birds frequent the perennial and seasonal swamps and the ephemeral pans, including darters, reed cormorants and African fish eagles as well as various herons, egrets, storks, terns and kingfishers, all of which feed on fish. At high flood levels the Chobe River also has seasonally inundated floodplains.

- **Ephemeral pans:** When the floods recede, ephemeral pans are left behind in depressions on the floodplain. These pans are often inhabited by stranded populations of air-breathing catfishes on which marabous and yellow-billed storks, African spoonbills and various herons and egrets, as well as scavenging mammals, such as hyaenas, feed. These pans may also be rain-filled pools in poorly drained clay soils associated with mopane woodland. When the ephemeral pans are filled again in the next flood season their waters are enriched by the droppings of the birds and mammals that have fed in the area.
- **Vleis:** Vleis are shallow wetlands with silty substrates and abundant emergent plants. They form diverse habitats for a variety of small fish species and their prey.
- **Bogs and marshes:** These habitats occur on the fringes of the perennial swamp and have silt or mud substrates and luxuriant plant growth, with very little open water for fish to inhabit. Some small and hardy species make a living there, such as Johnston's topminnow and the Thamalakane barb.

Habitat preferences

Some Okavango fishes, such as pink bream, Okavango tilapia, spiny eels, labyrinths, snoutfishes, tigerfish and pike, have very specific habitat requirements, while others are widely distributed within the various habitats of the delta. In most species the habitat preferences of the fry and juveniles differ from those of the adults, with the earlier life-history stages typically sharing their habitat with the adults of other, smaller species.

Habitat under water lily beds   Underwater habitat in a bed of water chestnuts

The largest differentiation in terms of habitat preferences is between species that are best equipped to survive in more stable, perennial waterbodies, such the main river channel, riverine panhandle and permanent lagoons, and those that are better equipped to live in relatively unstable and seasonally flooded habitats, such as the backwater lagoons, side channels, drainage rivers and floodplains.

Species that are equipped for extreme environments, such as killifishes and some of the air-breathing catfishes, are able to penetrate ephemeral, intermittently flooded waterbodies *(mulapos)* and lakes that are prone to drying up, like Lake Ngami. Some very adaptable species, such as the copperstripe barb, hyphen barb and red barb, have the ability to live in a variety of habitats, from the edges of perennial swamps and channels to backwater lagoons, floodplains and the rivers that drain water out of the swamps.

Within a waterbody many species prefer living on the bottom, such as most catfishes, spiny eels and snoutfishes, whereas others, like the top predators and some large cyprinids, prefer midwater habitats. A few species, especially the topminnows and some small cyprinids, choose to live near the water surface. Some habitat specialists, such as the multibar and broadbar citharines, live among dense reed and papyrus mats and rootstocks. In the perennial swamp and along the edges of permanent channels, where the underside of the enormous floating papyrus mats forms an unusual habitat that provides shelter over deep water, habitat specialists, such as the dwarf stonebasher, blackspot climbing perch, longtail spiny eel and ocellated spiny eel live.

Some species undertake regular migrations from one part of the delta to another, often in response to the rains or floods, or between habitats, to find new feeding grounds or places that are suitable for breeding. Other species, such as the sharptooth and blunttooth catfishes, migrate along the fringes of the receding floodplain to catch snoutfishes and other species that are forced into deeper water. Some of the top predators, such as tigerfish and pike, lurk on the edge of the receding floodplain for the same reason.

Feeding behaviour and predator-prey relationships

As in any seasonal wetland system, the fishes are divided into three main feeding groups or guilds:
- predators,
- herbivores and
- detritivores.

The great majority of Okavango Delta and Chobe River fishes are predators, i.e. they eat live animals, mainly insects, crabs, shrimps, snails and other fishes. Some of the larger predators are piscivorous once mature, feeding almost exclusively on fish and may also take frogs, small reptiles such as snakes, and even small birds and mammals. Some of the larger predators may be cannibals that will eat smaller specimens of their own species if they can catch them. Small predators, such as the topminnows, may feed on insects that fall on the water surface.

Only one fish in the Okavango Delta and Chobe River – the redbreast tilapia – feeds mainly on higher plants, although it also eats insects and crustaceans; but many feed on algae and diatoms, which are lower plants.

Many bottom-living species feed on detritus, which comprises decomposed material, but they also eat living diatoms, algae, bacteria and other micro-organisms. Some detritivores show a preference for lagoons that are frequented by hippos, as their copious dung creates a 'eutrophic' environment – one with very high nutrient levels – in which a rich detritus develops.

A few species, such as the silver catfish and squeakers, are omnivores in that they feed on both plants and animals, and some, such as the sharptooth and blunttooth catfishes, feed on a wide variety of foods, including carrion, i.e. the decomposing carcasses of large, dead animals, when available.

B. van der Waal

Migrating sharptooth catfish jumping the Popa Rapids

Breeding strategies

Broadly, fishes have three breeding strategies and are divided into:
- non-guarders,
- guarders, and
- bearers.

Non-guarders release their eggs and sperm into the water, where fertilization takes place. The eggs then drift in midwater or settle on the substrate or on plants, where they are left to develop unprotected. Some non-guarders (called 'brood hiders') hide their fertilized eggs under sand, logs or leaves but do not guard them.

Guarders protect their developing eggs and young in a nest, which may be a hollow scooped out in the sand, or a foam nest, whereas **bearers** protect their eggs and young in a body cavity such as the mouth (external bearers) or oviduct (internal bearers).

Non-guarders in the Okavango Delta comprise 58 species (65% of all species) and include all cyprinids, citharines, robbers, tigerfish, catfishes, spiny eels, topminnows, the killifish and one of the labyrinth species.

M. Bruton

Male sharptooth catfish chasing a female during courtship and prior to mating

R. Bills

Foam nest of the Southern African pike

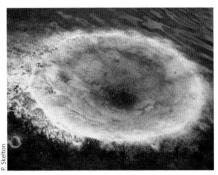

P. Skelton

Sandy hollow nest of the threespot tilapia, *Oreochromis andersonii*

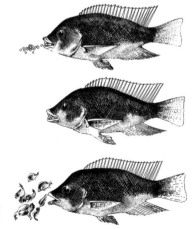

L. Voigt

Oreochromis species guard their eggs and young in their mouth.

The humpback cichlid *Serranochromis altus* is an example of a mouthbrooding fish in the Okavango Delta.

Guarders comprise 17 species (19%) and include the snoutfishes, pike, jewelfishes, the banded, Okavango and redbreast tilapias, and one of the labyrinth species.

Bearers comprise 14 species (16%) and include most of the cichlids (southern mouthbrooder, breams, sargos, largemouth breams and *Oreochromis* species), all of which protect their eggs and young in their mouths (external bearers). There are no internal bearers in the Okavango Delta, unless the potentially invasive alien mosquitofish, live-bearer or guppy are found to occur there.

The parental investment in each young, i.e. how much energy is invested in each individual egg or fry by the parents, differs widely according to the breeding strategy. It is lowest in non-guarders, which produce large numbers of small eggs, and highest in bearers, which produce small numbers of large eggs, with guarders displaying intermediate investment.

The three broad categories of breeding strategy are divided into 29 breeding guilds, of which 18 occur in the Okavango Delta. This is a very high diversity of breeding strategies compared to the fishes of the African Great Lakes (such as Lake Malawi), which have only four breeding guilds and are dominated (over 92%) by one guild (mouth-brooding cichlids). The reason that the Okavango Delta has such a wide diversity of breeding strategies is because it includes both stable habitats – such as the riverine panhandle and perennial swamps and lagoons – which favour the survival of guarders and bearers, as well as unstable habitats – such as seasonal swamps and *mulapos* – which favour non-guarders.

Fish that have a low risk/high investment strategy are more likely to survive in more stable environments where they must compete for resources with many other species. In contrast, those that have a high risk/low investment strategy are more successful in unstable environments where there is less competition between species, as mortalities there are caused mainly by catastrophic environmental events over which they have no control.

Survival tactics

Fishes living in swamps and rivers face many threats to their survival, especially from desiccation and predation. Those species that live in habitats that dry out seasonally, such as shallow floodplains, ephemeral pools and even lakes like Lake Ngami, have anatomical and behavioural adaptations that allow them to survive those conditions. As the waters recede after the flood, floodplain fishes migrate into deeper water and see out the dry season by sheltering in the fringes of reeds or papyrus growing in backwater lagoons and channels. Other species find shelter in the rootstocks and mats of papyrus floating over deeper water.

Caprivi killifish, like other killifishes, produce eggs that survive desiccation by being encased in dried mud. When the rains return, or the *mulapo* is flooded, the eggs hatch and the fry grow very quickly, as they need to complete their life cycle within a few months.

The air-breathing clariid catfishes, especially the sharptooth and blunttooth catfishes, have an air-breathing organ formed from a modified gill arch that allows them to survive habitat desiccation. When their gills become clogged with mud they use only their air-breathing organs for respiration. Because they can breathe air, they are able to migrate across wet ground in search of new habitats, their pectoral spines serving as 'legs'.

Air-breathing catfishes undertake massive feeding migrations in the Okavango Delta.

The two climbing perches have an air-breathing organ in a chamber above the gills that allows them to extract oxygen from the air. They can therefore survive in stagnant water with little oxygen and also shuffle across wet land after rain to find food or new habitats.

The fry of southern African pike cling to the underside of their foam nest to avoid predation by aerial predators, such as birds, while sand catlets hide under sand to avoid predators (and to ambush their prey).

An important survival tactic among fish is that egg, fry, juvenile and adult usually live in different habitats and face divergent threats. They therefore adopt different survival strategies at various stages of their life history. Most young fish shelter among plants or bottom sediments in shallow water and use camouflage, hiding behaviour and fast-swimming movements to avoid predators, whereas adults use their speed, strength and rapid reaction times to survive, or are active at low light levels.

Rare and endangered fishes

Most Okavango Delta and Chobe River fishes have wide distributions in rivers, swamps and floodplains to the north, east and south, and the species to which they belong are not threatened with extinction. Within the Okavango and Chobe, some species, such as the nembwe, threespot tilapia and greenhead tilapia, are overexploited and their numbers have been severely depleted, which means that they are probably unable to play their full ecological roles in the ecosystem and are poorly represented in the catches of traditional fishermen and anglers.

Many of the fishes featured in this book reach their southern limit of distribution in the Okavango Delta, which is a World Heritage Site. Some of these fishes, such as the Okavango suckermouth, Okavango churchill and Okavango tilapia, are in danger of having their ranges reduced in the catchments to the north, which may cause them to become rare or endangered.

The only Okavango or Chobe fish species that is listed as 'Endangered' in the IUCN's Red Data Book is the Caprivi killifish, as road building and pollution threaten its only known habitat. At present two Okavango and Chobe species, threespot tilapia and greenhead tilapia, are listed as 'Vulnerable' in the Red Data Book.

Moremi Game Reserve provides a safe refuge for many Okavango fishes, although they obviously also range well beyond its borders. The Chobe River forms a small section of the northern border of the Chobe National Park but the park provides little actual protection for the fishes living there.

The key to conserving the fishes of the Okavango Delta and Chobe River is preserving the natural hydrological cycle and habitats of intact fish communities, as opposed to just protecting threatened or endangered species. They will best be conserved by protective legislation and actions to ensure that the entire ecosystem in which they live continues to function normally in the long term. Fortunately, Botswana's authorities have recently introduced effective legislation to protect fish outside formally protected areas.

For more about the utilization and conservation of the Okavango Delta and Chobe River, see 'Utilization and Conservation', p. 111.

The key to the conservation of the fishes of the Okavango is to preserve the natural hydrological cycle. This photograph shows the seasonal swamp at high water level.

Angling in the Okavango

The sustainable use of Okavango fishes by anglers should be encouraged, as it promotes tourism, creates job opportunities and increases awareness of aquatic biodiversity and the overall ecology of the delta and adjacent river systems. However, angling efforts and yields need to be controlled so that they do not have a negative long-term impact on fish stocks and the functioning of aquatic ecosystems.

The frequency of angling competitions, in particular, needs to be carefully controlled, as substantially more fish are caught during these intensive events than during normal recreational fishing. Many angling competitions now encourage catch-and-release fishing, which is a positive move, although it may still cause stress-related mortalities in fish.

HINTS FOR ANGLERS

Tips on how to outwit fish are given in the species accounts for all species that are large enough to be of interest to anglers. Note that popular angling fish are indicated with an icon:

A few broad points that apply to most species are given here:
- You will be a more successful angler if you know your fishes, as you will learn when they are most vulnerable to your fishing method.
- Learn about their feeding preferences, preferred food size and feeding behaviour in this book and through your own field observations. Use this knowledge to select the best bait, hook size, fishing site and method.
- Learn about the timing of their homing and breeding migrations, the time of day (or night) when they are most active, where they prefer to hide, their habitat and depth preferences, and whether they prefer still or running water. Find out how the different species respond to water level changes before, during and after the flood, and even to overcast compared to clear skies.
- Remember that fish may shelter in one place but feed in another (like birds that roost in one place and feed in another), and that some species do not feed while they are digesting their food, nesting or migrating.
- Observe the behaviour of fishes and determine whether they prefer to feed at the water surface, in midwater or on the bottom. This will also help you to decide whether they prefer static or moving bait, and how fast you should retrieve your spinner or lure.
- Also learn about their anatomy, especially their mouth size and bite strength, and whether they are strong swimmers that are prone to leaping out of the water. This will help you to decide what kind of hook, trace and line to use.

- Remember that fish often take bait or chase lures that are very different from their natural food. While predators, such as tigerfish, pike and largemouths will be attracted by lures and spinners, detritivores that normally eat diatoms and detritus, such as *Oreochromis*, or algal grazers, like some cyprinids and squeakers, will take a baited hook. Although fish do not encounter porridge or mealie meal in nature they will readily take it as bait, partly because small pieces of bait diffuse into the water column and are detected by the fish.
- Observe the behaviour of natural fish predators, especially fish-eating birds, as they may provide hints on fish distribution and abundance.
- Use the lightest tackle and the smallest hook for a given fish species to even out the contest between 'predator' and prey and to ensure that you have to exercise some skill in landing your catch.
- Avoid using bright brass swivels, as tigerfish may attack them and cut your line.
- In general, in running water it is best to cast downstream and retrieve the lure or spinner upstream against the current.
- Be careful, while you are baiting your hook, that you don't leave human smells and tastes on the hook or line that might repel fish, as they have a very keen sense of taste. Some expert anglers rinse their hands in fish offal before handling their hook and line so as to obscure human chemicals. Anyone who has watched fish underwater approach a baited hook will know that they are very skittish about committing themselves to the take, and even the faintest strange chemical cue will cause them to retreat.
- If you are fishing from a boat, ensure that your line, hook or bait never falls into the bilges and becomes contaminated with oil or other foreign chemicals, as this might also repel fish.

Efimova Anna/Shutterstock.com

The tigerfish is one of the prime freshwater game fish in Africa.

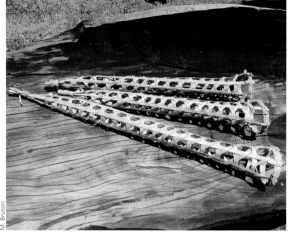

Constriction traps used by traditional fishermen to catch snake catfish   Young boy with a tigerfish catch

Anglers are encouraged to use catch-and-release methods and to do so in such a way that the fish suffers the least amount of stress, as an overstressed fish can die after release. Air-breathing catfishes, squeakers and some large cichlids are far more hardy than the tigerfish, which builds up lactic acid in its body through anaerobic metabolism during the vigorous fight, and often becomes fish eagle prey even if it is carefully removed from the hook and released immediately. Consideration should be given to using barbless hooks (as fly fishermen do), which cause less damage to the fish's mouth, for catch-and-release fishing. Excessive chumming of the water is discouraged as this may interfere with natural food cycles.

Anglers are encouraged to catch fish in moderation and only to meet their immediate needs. Also, remember that the only net that you can legally use without a permit is a landing net, and that it is important that you have a fishing permit if one is required. Anglers are encouraged to be humane towards their catch and to place fish that will be kept into live-bait baskets, or kill them, rather than allow them to die protracted deaths on land or in boats. Anglers should be respectful of the rights of other water users, especially traditional fishermen, whose livelihood, and that of their families, may depend on their daily fish catch.

Use your angling experience to develop a deeper appreciation for the beauty and complexity of the Okavango Delta and Chobe River; they are unique environments that you are privileged to visit. After all, catching fish is only one of the reasons why we go angling, as it brings serenity of mind and offers rare opportunities for contemplative thought. Angling is more a mind-set than a sport, and one often hears anglers say that the fishing was good, although the catch was poor. The supreme test of an angler is not how many fish he or she has caught, but how much he or she has benefited when they caught no fish. Angling is the most popular form of hunting in which modern humans engage, and it is becoming more popular every year but, if we overfish the stocks, everyone is a loser.

How to identify a fish

The typical characteristics of a fish species vary according to its age, sex and breeding condition, and may even vary at different times of day or night. A dying fish is very stressed and may be different in colour and appearance to a healthy fish. The following are key features to note when attempting to make an identification.

Body shape varies and may be:
- elongate and eel-like (as in the spiny eels) **(A)**
- elongate but deeper and shorter (clariid catfishes) **(B)**
- ellipsoid and fusiform (most cyprinids, alestids and other catfishes) **(C, D, E, F, H)**
- triangular as in squeakers **(G)**, or
- short and deep (many cichlids) **(H, I)**.

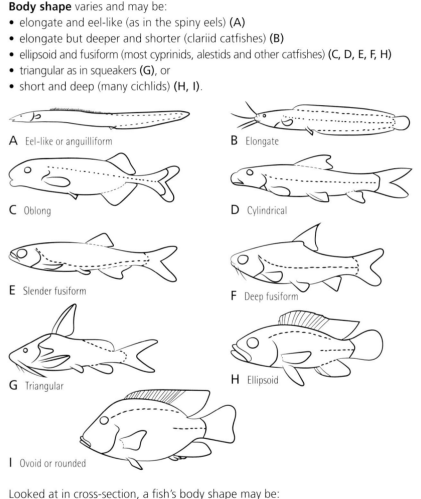

A   Eel-like or anguilliform

B   Elongate

C   Oblong

D   Cylindrical

E   Slender fusiform

F   Deep fusiform

G   Triangular

H   Ellipsoid

I   Ovoid or rounded

Looked at in cross-section, a fish's body shape may be:
- depressed (flattened and wide, as in sand catlets)
- triangular (squeakers)
- cylindrical (air-breathing catfishes), or
- compressed (flattened from side to side; silver catfish).

Many catfishes have flattened heads and compressed bodies and tails.

Head shape and structures are important identification aids. The slope of the head and forehead, nature and position of the nasal openings (nares), size and position of the eyes, size, shape and position of the mouth (**A, B, C**), and the nature of the teeth are important characters. The teeth may be:
• large and sharp for biting (as in predators),
• multi-cusped for cutting and chewing (omnivores), or
• small and arranged on tooth bands for grasping, grazing and grinding (many catfishes and alga feeders).
The gill cover and gill-slit openings can be diagnostic, as some are large (**A, B**) whereas others are short slits on the side of the head or are short and restricted to the sides (**C**). The sharp spikes on the opercles of the manyspined climbing perch allow it to shuffle over wet ground and are also diagnostic. The presence or absence, and length, of barbels is important to note, as well as whether they are simple (one filament, as in clariid catfishes) or branched (most squeakers).

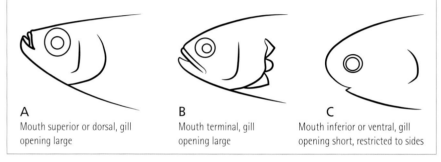

A
Mouth superior or dorsal, gill opening large

B
Mouth terminal, gill opening large

C
Mouth inferior or ventral, gill opening short, restricted to sides

Fins: (See 'External anatomy of a typical Okavango fish', p. 29) The position and shape of the fins is often an important diagnostic feature. The dorsal fin may have its origin far forward (as in many catfishes), in the middle of the body (many minnows) or behind the middle (southern African pike and topminnows). A second dorsal fin (adipose fin, which is fleshy and has no spines or rays) is characteristic of some catfishes and all distichodontids and alestids. The tail fin may have two lobes and be forked or lunate, or it may form one broad, paddle-like fin that has a straight edge, slightly indented edge (emarginate), slightly rounded edge (truncate) or a well-rounded hind margin. Tail fins may also be pointed or, in the case of spiny eels, sharply pointed. The size and position of the anal fin is important. Many mormyrids, alestids and catfishes have long anal fins whereas minnows have short anal fins and cichlids have anal fins that are intermediate in length.

The pectoral and pelvic fins are paired and their size and position are important diagnostic characters. The pectoral fins may be high on the body (as in cichlids, anabantids, silver catfish) or low down (most cyprinids, citharines, robbers, tigerfish, squeakers), or in an intermediate position (air-breathing catfishes, mormyrids). The pelvic fins of the spiny-rayed fishes (cichlids and anabantids) are far forward on the body, just behind the origin of the pectoral fins, whereas they are in midbody in most other fishes from the region. In general, fishes that have their pectoral fins high up on the body, and the pelvic fins far forward, are good at hovering and manoeuvring whereas the other fishes are typically faster swimmers.

Fin rays and spines: The fins are supported by rays (segmented cartilaginous struts) and spines (hard, bony spikes). Rays are either simple (unbranched) or branched, and may sometimes be modified into spines, as in catfishes and cyprinids, which typically have a single fin spine. Spiny-rayed fishes, like cichlids, spiny eels and anabantids, have a series of spines in the dorsal and anal fins. The number of spines and rays in the dorsal and anal fins is often diagnostic and is an important feature when identifying similar species. The fin spine-and-ray formula is given as Roman capitals (I, II, III…) for spines (or spinous rays) and Roman lower case (i, ii, iii…) for simple or branched rays. The fin formula for the leopard squeaker, which has one spine and seven rays in the dorsal fin and four branched rays and 8–10 unbranched rays in the anal fin, for example is therefore: D I, 7; A iv, 8–10.

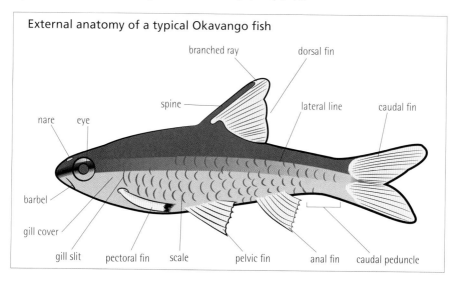

External anatomy of a typical Okavango fish

branched ray · dorsal fin · spine · lateral line · caudal fin · nare · eye · barbel · gill cover · gill slit · pectoral fin · scale · pelvic fin · anal fin · caudal peduncle

Scales: It is important to note whether the fish has scales (most do) or not (catfishes). It is also important to note whether there are scales on the head (as in cichlids, anabantids and cyprinodontids), or only on the body (mormyrids, cyprinids, alestids). If the fish has scales, what is the relative size of these scales? Are they tiny (as in spiny eels), small (most mormyrids), medium in size (cyprinids, alestids and anabantids), or fairly large (cichlids)? Scales may be either cycloid (simple and round or oval in shape with a smooth edge) or ctenoid (with fine teeth along the outer margin).

Scale size can be accurately assessed by counting rows of scales, either along the lateral line from the head to the base of the tail fin or, where there is no lateral line, along the length of the body (scale series). The number of scales between the lateral line and the base of the dorsal fin, or between the lateral line and the pelvic and anal fins, may also be counted, as well as the number of scale rows around the caudal peduncle. Sometimes special features of scales, such as enlarged scales at the base of a fin, are useful as an identification aid.

Lateral line: The lateral line, a sensory canal within the scales or skin, is a characteristic feature of most fishes in the Okavango Delta and Chobe River (p. 27, **A–F**). In the cichlids and anabantids the lateral line is divided into two sections: a high section near the front and a lower section towards the back (p. 27, **H–I**). Some fish species have a restricted, broken or interrupted lateral line (e.g. dwarf barb and some catfishes) and, in others, it is absent (spiny eels).

Colour: In life, many freshwater fishes are well camouflaged in broken patterns of dull and sombre black, grey, brown or olive. Countershading (dark above, light below) is also a common feature. Colours and pigment patterns are usually expressed more vividly in clear water, whereas in cloudy or turbid water they are suppressed, and silvery or faded colours are more common. Bright colours (red, blue, yellow and green) are important in breeding adult fishes, especially cichlids, cyprinids and topminnows, and serve to attract mates, but these colours fade quickly under stress or after death.

Pigment patterns include spots, blocks, irregular squiggles and dashes, bands and vertical and horizontal bars as well as speckling and shading. Special markings include 'eye-spots' on the rear end of a fish, such as the spottail barb, that might deflect a predator's attention away from the head. 'Egg-spots' on the anal fin of some cichlids simulate freshly laid eggs and encourage the male to release sperm and fertilize the eggs that the female has released from the genital pore near the anal fin. Some species (such as squeakers) show wide variations in pigment patterns within a species in different regions and it is important to realize this when you are trying to identify them (the teeth and barbels of squeakers may also vary within species).

Abbreviations used in the species accounts
- The scientific and English names are given for all species in the accounts that follow (pp. 32–110). Local names are included wherever possible (**B:** BaYei, **H:** Hambukushu, **S:** Setswana).
- Average length **(AL)** is the average length of a large sample of fish; standard length **(SL)** is the distance from the snout to the point of flexure (bending) of the tail fin and is used for fish in which the tail fin is often damaged; total length **(TL)** is the distance from the snout to the most posterior point of the tail fin in fish with square or round tails; fork length **(FL)** is the distance from the snout to the middle of the fork in fish with forked tails.

An aerial view of a river channel in the Okavango Delta

Unusual soft-bodied freshwater fishes distributed throughout the tropics in Africa. They have small scales, and in several species the snout is extended into a proboscis. Body colour silvery or brown, black or grey. Gill slits small. Dorsal and anal fins often extended, with many soft rays; narrow caudal peduncles, where the electric organ is found. Tail fins forked and rounded. Mormyrids are predators that usually hunt at night and can send and receive weak electric currents, which they use to communicate with one another and to detect predators or prey. Each species has a distinctive electrical discharge. Some mormyrids make sounds, have complex courtships and may build nests and guard their young. Some species migrate in large shoals at night. Eleven species are known from the region.

Cubango stonebasher   *Cyphomyrus cubangoensis* (Pellegrin, 1936)

Avg L: 80 mm, SL:100 mm; D 28–33; A 21–24. 45–48 scales in lateral series, 12–16 scales around the caudal peduncle. Deep, compressed body, back rounded. Dorsal fin long, origin before that of anal fin. Caudal peduncle slender, tail fin forked and rounded. Head rounded, with subterminal mouth, chin with fleshy bulge, eye well above mouth. Males with kink in anal fin and with anterior anal rays broader and longer than posterior rays, forming a bulge. Colour dark brown or black, with a black band between the dorsal and anal fins.

A nocturnal shoaling snoutfish that prefers vegetated, slow-flowing channels and lagoons and rocky rapids. Adults live in deeper river channels with soft substrates. This fish generates a weak electric field, using specialized skeletal muscles, to detect the small, bottom-living invertebrates on which it preys. After rain or floods it migrates from channels into newly flooded backwater lagoons and floodplains, possibly for breeding. Known from the Okavango Delta and Chobe River, and from the upper Zambezi River in the Zambezi Region of Namibia (formerly the Caprivi Strip). Protected by the relative inaccessibility of its preferred habitats.

Slender stonebasher   *Hippopotamyrus ansorgii* (Boulenger, 1905)

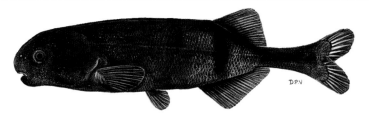

Avg L: 80–100 mm, SL: 150 mm; D 18–19; A 24–26. 16–21 scales around caudal peduncle. Body long, slender, compressed. Dorsal fin origin set far back and behind that of the anal fin. Caudal peduncle elongate, tail fin forked with rounded lobes. Head rounded with fleshy, terminal mouth. Body dark brown to black with a dark band between the dorsal and anal fins.

Uncommon. Favours flowing water in fringing papyrus, and reed rootstocks and rocky habitats in the riverine panhandle and further upstream. Nocturnal, feeding on small aquatic invertebrates such as insect larvae. Breeding occurs at night. Fairly common in the Kavango River between Andora Mission and Popa Rapids, but not recorded from the Chobe River. It is included here as it may occur in the perennial swamp of the Okavango Delta. No conservation measures in place, but is protected by the inaccessibility of its preferred habitats. Named after the explorer William John Ansorge (1850–1913), who collected the first specimens.

Szabo's stonebasher   *Hippopotamyrus szaboi* Kramer, Van der Bank & Wink, 2004

P. Skelton (NGOWP)

Avg L: 70–80 mm, SL: 100 mm; D 18–21; A 21–25. 17–22 scales around the caudal peduncle. Body long and slender, compressed. Head sloping, rounded, with a terminal mouth. Lower jaw bulges to below ventral line of body. Colour dark brown or black, with a dark band between the dorsal and anal fins.

Flowing-water snoutfish that inhabits papyrus and reed rootballs and rocky habitats in the upper Zambezi River in Namibia. Probably more widespread, but not yet confirmed from the Kavango or Kwando rivers. It is included here as it may occur in the perennial swamp of the Okavango Delta. Collected from the upper Zambezi River near Katima Mulilo, where it is found in rocky habitats in the main river channel. Nocturnal, feeding on small aquatic invertebrates such as insect larvae. Breeding takes place at night. Like other mormyrids, it has a unique 'electrical signature'. Named in honour of Thomas Szabo (1924–1993), pioneer in the study of electroreception in fishes.

Upper Zambezi bulldog
Marcusenius altisambesi Kramer, Skelton, Van der Bank & Wink, 2007
Nkungu (B)

G. Neef (NGOWP)

Avg L: 150–160 mm, SL: 195 mm; D 20–26; A 26–30. 49–60 scales in lateral series, 12–14 scales around the caudal peduncle. Body elongate and compressed. Dorsal and anal fins set far back. Caudal peduncle 2–3 times longer than deep. Chin a prominent elongate lobe. May be dark olive and grey with bronze flecks and dark brown blotches, or light golden brown.

A common and hardy snoutfish that is tolerant of low oxygen and high turbidity levels and is often one of the last remaining species in drying waterbodies. This shoaling fish is common in well-vegetated, muddy-bottomed habitats in slow-flowing rivers, such as the lower Boro, as well as in lagoons and flooded sawgrass floodplains. When water levels are low, it finds refuge in perennial floodplain lagoons, such as Dungu and Gomuto. A major source of prey for catfishes during the annual catfish runs, as the catfish use their barbels to detect the bulldog's electrical discharges. Feeds on aquatic invertebrates, especially insect larvae, and breeds during the rainy season in well-vegetated, newly flooded shallows. It is distributed throughout the Okavango Delta and Chobe River as well as in the upper Zambezi River system. Caught by subsistence fishermen using hook-and-line gear and traditional fish traps.

Western bottlenose
Mormyrus lacerda Castelnau, 1861
Nkungu (B)

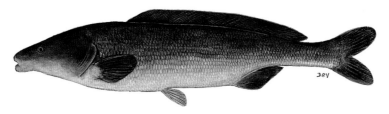

Avg L: 350–400 mm, TL: 500 mm; D 62–68; A 18–21. 80–90 scales in lateral series. Body elongate and compressed. Dorsal fin more than twice as long as anal fin. Tail fin forked with rounded lobes, partially scaled. Snout tapers downwards, mouth small and terminal. Grey-brown above, lighter and yellowish below. Reaches 2 kg.

The largest snoutfish in the Okavango Delta. Inhabits slower-flowing river channels, backwater lagoons and floodplains with aquatic vegetation and soft substrates. Nocturnal, feeding on insect larvae, crabs, snails and small fish. It breeds in inundated shallows and slow-flowing river channels during the summer rainy season, after the annual flood. Distributed throughout the Okavango Delta and Chobe River, which is the southern limit of its distribution. Also found in the upper Zambezi, Kafue and Cunene rivers. Protected in the Moremi Game Reserve and Chobe National Park. Caught by subsistence fishermen and occasionally by anglers using a hook and line. Named in honour of the Portuguese explorer and astronomer Francisco José Maria de Lacerda (1753–1798).

Long-head churchill   *Petrocephalus longicapitis* Kramer, Bills, Skelton & Wink, 2012

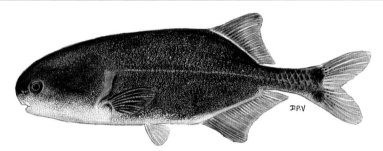

Avg L: 80–100 mm, SL: 110mm; D 21–25; A 26–30. 37–39 scales in lateral series, 12 scales around the slender caudal peduncle. Body oval. Anal fin longer than dorsal fin. Hind margin of dorsal and anal fins crescent-shaped, tail fin forked with rounded lobes. Males with a kink in the anal fin base. Head long and ellipsoid, rounded in front. Mouth small and ventral. Body silver-grey, underside lighter; paired fins transparent. Indistinct dark spot below anterior base of dorsal fin.

This species inhabits the margins of small river channels, floodplains and lagoons. Favours dense vegetation and a sand, gravel or rocky substrate. Feeds on insect larvae and other small invertebrates. Breeds during the summer rainy season in newly flooded shallows and slow-flowing river channels. Distributed widely in the Okavango Delta and Chobe River as well as in the upper Zambezi River system, although it is not abundant. The southern limit of its distribution is the Okavango Delta. Caught by subsistence fishermen using traditional fish traps.

Large-bodied churchill   *Petrocephalus magnitrunci* Kramer, Bills, Skelton & Wink, 2012

G. Neef (NGOWP)

Avg L: 70–75 mm, SL: 89 mm; D 0, 19–22; A 0, 27–31. 39–41 scales in lateral series, 11–12 scales around the caudal peduncle. Body oval. Anal fin longer than dorsal fin, tail fin forked with rounded lobes, caudal peduncle slender. Males with a kink in the anal fin base. Head rounded, with a small ventral mouth. Colour dark brown to grey or olive, no black spot below dorsal fin.

A recently described species of churchill that is characteristic of the Okavango Delta. Inhabits shallow floodplain lagoons that are inundated during the flood cycle and dry out over the low-water period. These lagoons have soft, muddy substrates and dense emergent plants, including sawgrasses and water lilies (*Nymphaea* spp.). Feeds on insect larvae and other small invertebrates. Breeds in newly inundated floodplains and slow-flowing river channels during the summer rainy season, after the arrival of the flood. Protected in the Moremi Game Reserve.

Okavango churchill   *Petrocephalus okavangoensis* Kramer, Bills, Skelton & Wink, 2012

G. Neef (NGOWP)

Avg L: 70–75 mm, SL: 95 mm; D 20–24; A 27–32. 37–38 scales in lateral series, 12 scales around the caudal peduncle. Body compressed. Dorsal and anal fins set far back, hind edges emarginate or crescent-shaped, especially in adults. Head with an angular profile. Colour silvery grey with golden-olive hue. Black spot below dorsal fin, not always prominent. Dark line along the base of the tail fin. Anterior dorsal and anal fin rays usually dark grey to black.

A hardy snoutfish that inhabits well-vegetated, soft-bottomed habitats in slow-flowing rivers, lagoons and sawgrass floodplains, and papyrus rootstocks in the perennial swamp. Feeds on invertebrates, especially insect larvae. Perennial floodplain lagoons in the riverine panhandle, such as Dungu and Gomuto, serve as refuges during low-water periods. This churchill is an important prey species during the annual catfish runs in the riverine panhandle. Breeds in newly inundated areas and channels during the summer rainy season, after the arrival of the annual flood. Males defend territories using sounds and electric signals to communicate. Protected in the Moremi Game Reserve. Found only in the Okavango Delta, upstream in the Kavango River in Namibia and in the Cubango River in Angola.

Dwarf stonebasher   *Pollimyrus castelnaui* (Boulenger, 1911)

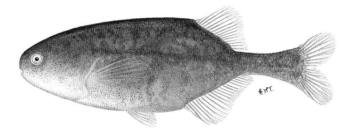

Avg L: <55–60 mm, SL: 70 mm; D 16–18; A 22–26. 46–53 scales along body, usually 12 scales around the caudal peduncle. Body oval and compressed. Dorsal fin base shorter than anal fin base. Tail fin forked and rounded. Mouth small and subterminal, chin without a swelling. Colour mottled brown.

This is the smallest snoutfish in the Okavango Delta and Chobe systems. It lives in a wide range of habitats, from the densely vegetated margins of river channels to floodplain lagoons. Nocturnal, feeding on aquatic insect larvae, especially the nymphs of midges (chironomids). Its common name refers to its small size and aggressive feeding action. Breeds in newly inundated shallows and slow-flowing river channels during the summer rainy season, after the arrival of the annual flood. Communicates using sound and electric signals. Emits electric discharges in five phases, of moderate duration. Distributed throughout the Kavango and Chobe systems and in other systems to the north. Protected in the Moremi Game Reserve and Chobe National Park. First described from Lake Ngami and named in honour of the French naturalist Francis de Castelnau (1810–1880), who described several new fish species from Lake Ngami.

Cuando dwarf stonebasher
Pollimyrus cuandoensis Kramer, Van der Bank & Wink, 2013

N. Mazungula (NGOWP)

Avg L: <60 mm, SL: 65 mm; D 15–18; A 23–25. Usually 14 scales around the caudal peduncle. Body oblong. Origin of anal fin in front of origin of dorsal fin. Caudal peduncle slender, tail fin forked and rounded. Head rounded with a small, terminal mouth. Colour mottled dark brown or black, throat lighter with fine spots.

This newly described snoutfish lives along the well-vegetated margins of river channels and in seasonal floodplains. Feeds on aquatic invertebrates and breeds in newly inundated areas and slow-flowing channels during the summer rainy season, after the arrival of the annual floods. Only known from the Kwando River upstream of Linyanti and not as yet recorded from the Kavango or Chobe systems, although it may occur there. Does not occur in the Moremi Game Reserve or Chobe National Park. Its electric discharges are in five phases, of very short duration. A recent study of *Pollimyrus* species in the region has revealed that the Cuando dwarf stonebasher differs from Zambezi dwarf stonebasher (Zambezi River system) and the dwarf stonebasher (Kavango and Chobe systems) in aspects of its anatomy and in the nature of its electric organ discharges.

Zambezi dwarf stonebasher
Pollimyrus marianne Kramer, Van der Bank, Flint, Sauer-Gürth & Wink, 2003

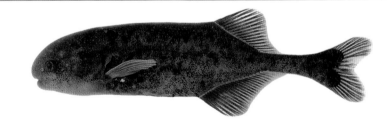

D. Tweddle

Avg L: <60 mm, SL: 65 mm; D 14–19; A 21–26. Usually 16 scales around the caudal peduncle. Body flattened. Anal fin origin in front of that of dorsal fin. Tail fin forked and rounded, with lobes overlapping. Caudal peduncle slender. Head rounded with a small, terminal mouth. Colour dark, with heavy grey or black mottling.

Inhabits the fast-flowing reaches of rocky rapids in rivers as well as dense reed beds over sandy substrates in backwaters. Known only from the lower reaches of the upper Zambezi system, but probably occurs in the Chobe River. It is difficult to distinguish from other stonebashers by its general morphology, but its electrical discharges are longer than those of the dwarf or Cuando dwarf stonebashers with a three-phase pattern that distinguishes this species from closely related stonebashers in the area. It has an elaborate courtship and builds a nest where it guards its eggs and young. Named in honour of Marianne Elfriede Kramer, mother of electroreception researcher, Berndt Kramer.

BARBS, MINNOWS, YELLOWFISHES AND LABEOS Cyprinidae

A large family of freshwater fishes with over 1,600 species in Africa, Europe, Asia and North America. Over 475 species occur in Africa, with 80 species in southern Africa. They vary widely in size, shape, lifestyle and habitat; many are strong swimmers living in fast-flowing water. They lack teeth on their jaws but have teeth on their pharyngeal (throat) bones. They lack a true stomach but, especially in the detritus and plant feeders, have extended, convoluted guts. Some species have barbels. They have one dorsal fin, pelvic fins in midbody and a forked tail fin. Males may differ from females in having longer fins, different colour patterns and tubercles on the head. Nine species known from the region. Southern African barbs that were previously in the genus *Barbus* are now placed in the genus *Enteromius*.

Redeye labeo   *Labeo cylindricus* Peters, 1852

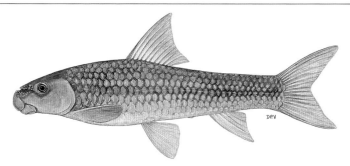

SL: 230 mm; D iii, 9–10; A iii, 5. Scales moderate in size, 34–37 in lateral line, 12–16 (usually 14) around the caudal peduncle, five scale rows between the lateral line and dorsal fin. Body slender and cylindrical. Dorsal fin moderately tall, tail fin forked. Head has prominent snout with star-shaped tubercles. Eyes on upper side of head. Mouth large, below snout. Outer lips fleshy, inner rims with a horny sharp edge. Inner surface of lips lined with small papillae. Single pair of small barbels. Colour varies from olive or brown to golden-green with a dark lateral band. Larger specimens usually darker olive-grey, eye red above, belly light olive-brown to off-white. Males smaller and more slender than females. Reaches sexual maturity at about 100 mm SL and attains 230mm SL. Reaches 0.9 kg.

The smallest labeo in southern Africa. A streamlined fish that favours clear, running water in rocky habitats in small and large rivers. One of the few species that is able to survive in open waters in the company of tigerfish, from which it hides in rocky crevices. The mouth is adapted for grazing on algae and detritus on the river floor and on the surfaces of rocks and logs, where it leaves characteristic grazing tracks. May also graze on exposed fungal infections on other fishes and from the skin of hippos. Redeye labeos are strong swimmers that often congregate in large shoals and migrate upstream against strong currents in order to breed. In Lake Malawi, they lay their eggs among rocks; their breeding cycle in the Okavango Delta is unknown, although it is likely to coincide with the summer rainy season and the annual floods. In turbulent water, such as in rapids, they are able to use their sucker-like mouths and broad pectoral fins to clamber over damp rocks and low weirs. This labeo is found in perennial river channels and lagoons in the northern Okavango Delta, and upstream into the riverine reaches of the Kavango River in Namibia and the Cubango River in Angola. Also occurs in the Chobe River. Protected in the Moremi Game Reserve and Chobe National Park. Elsewhere it is found in the Zambezi, Zambian Congo and Lualaba systems and beyond, in central and east Africa, southwards through the Zambezi River system and east coast rivers to the Phongolo system in KwaZulu-Natal. A minor component of the subsistence fishery due to its preference for fast-flowing water. In an aquarium, keeps the glass clean by grazing on algae. Not generally considered an angling species, it can be taken on a small hook using a pellet of mealie meal as bait. Excellent bait for predatory fishes.

Upper Zambezi labeo   *Labeo lunatus* Jubb, 1963
Didove (H), *Nkokokoya* (B)

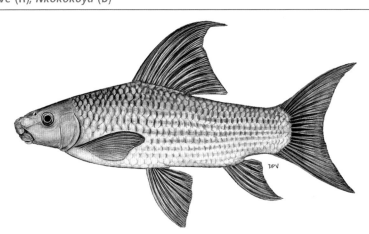

SL: 400 mm; D iv, 9–11; A iii, 5. 37–40 scales in lateral line, 16–20 around a deep caudal peduncle. Body deep, broadest in the middle and tapered at both ends. Dorsal fin tall and crescent-shaped, tail fin large, pectoral fin with black leading edge. Snout with weak tubercles, mouth with fleshy lips and sharp-edged horny inner rims, eye red. Upper body greenish or silvery grey, silvery below. Scale bases dark grey and form parallel lines along the body. Fin membranes grey. Reaches 2.5 kg.

This large labeo, with its distinctive crescent-shaped dorsal fin, inhabits a wide range of habitats in the Okavango Delta, including shallow, well-vegetated river channels such as the lower Boro and Boteti rivers, and large, soft-bottomed backwater lagoons such as the Maqwexana Pools in Moremi Game Reserve. Uncommon in the seasonal delta, but has been caught in the Thamalakane River near Matlapaneng. In the Kavango River in Namibia and Cubango River in Angola these fish inhabit rocky rapids. They feed on algae and detritus and are commonly encountered around hippos, where waters are naturally enriched. In summer they migrate upstream in shoals to spawn, laying their eggs among aquatic plants on recently inundated floodplains.

Juvenile fish live on the receding floodplains, where they are caught in large numbers in traditional traps set in fish weirs. This labeo is found throughout the Okavango Delta and Chobe River as well as in the upper Zambezi and Kafue systems. Not an important angling species, but adults can be caught on light tackle using earthworms or mealie meal pellets as bait. Protected in the Moremi Game Reserve and Chobe National Park. The southern limit of their distribution is the Okavango Delta. The first specimens were collected just above Victoria Falls by Rex Jubb, in 1963.

Upper Zambezi yellowfish   *Labeobarbus codringtonii* (Boulenger, 1908)

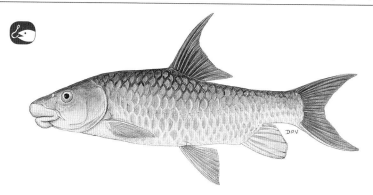

TL: 390 mm; D iii–iv, 9–10; A iii, 5. Scales large, 29–32 in lateral line, 12 around the caudal peduncle. Body robust. First dorsal ray flexible, dorsal fin tall, tail forked. Head large, mouth terminal, two pairs of barbels. Lips frequently thickened into 'rubberlips'. Colour gold-orange to olive, with the large scales lined in grey, fins dark grey, juveniles silvery olive-grey. Reaches 3.2 kg.

Rarely encountered, this species is nevertheless common in its habitat, i.e. fast-flowing, open water running over cobble or rocky substrates, especially rocky rapids. It seldom occurs over sand or in aquatic vegetation. It is a powerful swimmer with large fins that enable it to manoeuvre in fast-flowing water. Omnivorous, feeding on aquatic insect larvae, crustaceans, snails and small fish. Breeding habits unknown, but it probably spawns in the rainy season and after the arrival of the annual floodwaters. Found only in the upper Zambezi and Kavango systems. Does not occur in Moremi but may occur in the Chobe National Park.

A popular angling fish in the Kavango River in Namibia, it can be caught in open, running water using artificial flies, or grasshoppers as 'wet flies', or with a small silver spoon in deep pools below rocky rapids. A minor component of the subsistence fishery due to its preference for fast-flowing water. Named after Tom Codrington who collected fish near Victoria Falls in 1907.

Upjaw barb *Coptostomabarbus wittei* David & Poll, 1937
Masaradina (B)

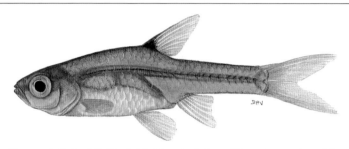

SL: 40 mm; D ii, 7; A ii–iii, 5. 26–29 scales in lateral line, 12 around caudal peduncle. Body arched, eyes large, caudal peduncle elongate. Scales thin and radiately striated, like those of other small barbs. Mouth small, terminal and upturned; no barbels. Body translucent pink, turning rose-red in the breeding season, belly silver-white. Thin stripe from head to tail, black triangle at base of the dorsal fin. Breeding males have tubercles on their snouts and are smaller and more slender than the females.

The upjaw barb inhabits shallow, densely vegetated, still-water habitats in swamps, floodplains and backwater lagoons, as well as the fringes of fast-flowing channels, but is not found in open water. Often found together with the sickle-fin barb. Migrates upstream along the fringes of rivers and may be caught in large numbers when river channels overflow onto the adjacent floodplains. Moves onto the floodplains to breed in summer, laying its eggs among submerged plants. In the riverine panhandle breeding takes place mainly in February. Feeds on plankton, insect larvae and algae on plant stems. Found throughout the Okavango Delta and Chobe River. Elsewhere occurs in the upper Zambezi, Kafue and Zambian Congo systems. Caught by traditional fishermen using woven baskets and traps.

Spottail barb *Enteromius afrovernayi* (Nichols & Boulton, 1927)
Masaradina (B)

SL: 57 mm; D III, 7; A iii, 5. 27–33 scales in lateral series, lateral line restricted to the first 3–7 scales only, 12 scales around the caudal peduncle. Body elongate with a small, upturned, terminal mouth, barbels absent. First dorsal spine serrated. Body narrows at anal fin. Colour translucent grey-brown to yellow with iridescent lilac-yellow stripe along body, silvery to transparent below; stripe becomes more prominent in dead specimens. Large black spot at base of forked tail fin.

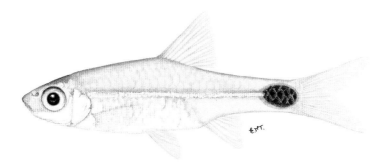

A common small barb that inhabits quiet, slow-flowing vegetated river channels, floodplains and backwater lagoons throughout the Okavango Delta but is more common in the perennial upper reaches. Feeds on small aquatic insects on the water surface or on algae attached to plants. Breeds between September and March during the summer rainy season, depositing the eggs on dense submerged vegetation. Spottail barbs in the perennial swamp spawn before those in the seasonal swamp. Found in the Kavango, Chobe, Cunene, upper Zambezi, Kafue and Congo systems. Caught by subsistence fishermen in fishing baskets. Attractive aquarium species. Named after Arthur S. Vernay, an American who sponsored several expeditions to Central Africa in the 1920s and 30s.

Blackback barb   *Enteromius barnardi* (Jubb, 1965)
Masaradina (B)

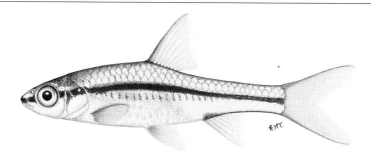

SL: 70 mm; D iii, 8; A iii, 5. 29–33 scales in lateral line, 12 scales around the caudal peduncle. Body slender with a small mouth at the end of a pointed snout. One pair of short, almost transparent barbels. Body silver-olive with silver on the sides and belly, fins pale yellow. Curved stripe from snout to tail that may be broken into black dots. Irregular black spots along the mid-back and a spot on the anal fin base. Breeding males have tubercles on their snouts and are smaller and more slender than females.

A small and abundant barb that inhabits shallow, well-vegetated streams, river edges, floodplains and marshes. Feeds on small insects and algae on plant stems. Predators include small tigerfish, southern African pike and sharptooth catfish. Migrates up streams or onto floodplains to breed during summer, laying its eggs among plants. Distributed throughout the Okavango Delta and Chobe River. Elsewhere found in the Kavango, Cunene, upper Zambezi, Kafue and Congo systems. Named by Rex Jubb after Keppel Barnard, who was Director of the South African Museum, Cape Town, from 1946 to 1956. First found on a fish farm in the Kafue River system. An attractive aquarium species.

Barotse barb   *Enteromius barotseensis* (Pellegrin, 1920)
Masaradina (B)

SL: 50 mm; D iii, 7–8; A iii, 5–6. Body cylindrical. 25–29 scales in lateral line, 12 around the caudal peduncle. Barbels short. Body has three or four black spots along the side, with additional spot at base of anal fin. Brown on upper body, silvery below, eye reddish above.

Inhabits slow-flowing channels and calm shallow backwaters amongst vegetation. Feeds on detritus, algae and small aquatic invertebrates. Ripe adults undertake upstream spawning migrations in spring or summer, after the first floods. Distributed throughout the Okavango Delta, in the Kavango River in Namibia and in the Cubango River in Angola, but not recorded from the Chobe River. Elsewhere it is found in the Cunene, Kafue and upper Zambezi systems. Also known from the southern tributaries of the Congo River. Caught in the subsistence fishery. A potential aquarium species.

Hyphen barb   *Enteromius bifrenatus* (Fowler, 1935)
Masaradina (B)

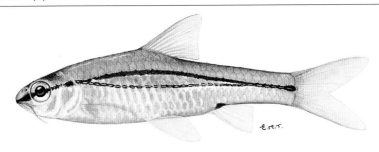

SL: 70 mm; D iii, 8; A iii, 5. 28–32 scales in lateral line, 12 around the caudal peduncle. Body slender with a small terminal mouth. Two pairs of long barbels. Two distinct black stripes along the body, one starting at the snout and running through the eye and gill cover and across the body to the tail, the other, thinner and curved, follows lateral line from behind head. Main body stripe may be broken into dashes. Olive-green above, silvery below, with fishes in turbid water darker. Black spot at base of anal fin. Dorsal and tail fins darker than other fins. Spawning males golden with orange fins. Lateral line tubules outlined in black.

A small barb found throughout the Okavango Delta in well-vegetated, slow-flowing river channels, floodplains, lagoons and backwater lagoons but not in open water. Also found in the main Kavango River during the low flood but uncommon in the headwater reaches. Common in the perennially flooded areas of the upper delta and upstream into Namibia but uncommon in the seasonal delta. Feeds on detritus, filamentous algae, seeds, aquatic invertebrates and insect larvae, such as caddis flies and mayflies. An important prey species for African pike, largemouth cichlids and catfish. Swims upriver to breed among flooded grasses after rain in summer, and after the arrival of the annual flood. Lays eggs on submerged roots and plant stems. Distributed throughout the Kavango, Chobe, Cunene, upper Zambezi, Kafue, Zambian Congo and Limpopo systems. Caught in traps by subsistence fishermen. First described from the Chobe River by H.W. Fowler.

Dwarf barb   *Enteromius brevidorsalis* (Boulenger, 1915)
Masaradina (B)

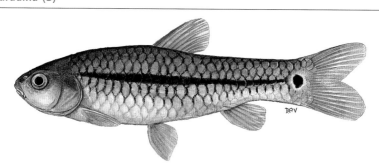

TL: 46 mm; D iii, 7; A iii, 5. 24–27 scales in lateral line, 11–14 around the caudal peduncle. Body short and rounded, the smallest barb in the region. Dorsal fin short (hence the specific name). Lateral line restricted to a few scales. Black stripe along the body ends in a black spot at the base of the tail fin. Light olive-yellow to olive-salmon above the lateral line, silvery below.

A small species, common in sawgrass-covered floodplain habitats, including backwater lagoons that are seasonally connected to perennial river channels. It is often the only cyprinid found in densely vegetated swampy habitats where little or no open water exists. Also found in slow-flowing river channels during the low flood cycle. Occurs in the Chobe, Kavango and Cubango systems but scarce in the perennial upper Okavango Delta and absent from the seasonal swamps. Elsewhere it is found in swamps and forest streams in the upper Zambezi, Kafue, Quanza and Congo systems. Caught by subsistence fishermen using fishing baskets and circular reed traps.

Orange-fin barb *Enteromius eutaenia* (Boulenger, 1904)
Masaradina (B)

SL: 140 mm; D III, 8; A iii, 5. 24–27 scales along the lateral line, 12 scales around the caudal peduncle. Large black scales at base of dorsal fin. Body stout with a large mouth and two pairs of barbels. Dorsal spine serrated. Bright or dark olive or brown above, silvery-white below, fins yellow or orange. Broad black stripe (sometimes wavy) runs from the snout to the tail, with shadow stripes on either side.

A flowing-water specialist that occurs almost exclusively in fast-flowing river channels and along river banks. Also inhabits papyrus and reed rootstocks and rocky and cobble habitats. Hunts for insects, but also grazes on filamentous algae and diatoms on plants and rocks. Breeds after rain on recently inundated floodplains. Most common in the panhandle and upstream in the Kavango (Namibia) and Cubango (Angola) rivers, but also found in perennial lagoons, such as Gadikwe, Xakanaxa and Xobecqa. Recorded in the Xo Lagoons on the Boro River and Qorokwe Lagoon on the Mborogha/Santandidbe rivers but not further southwards. Also found in the Chobe River and adjacent lagoons, as well as in Lake Tanganyika and the Cunene, Congo and Zambezi systems and southwards to the Phongolo River. Uncommon in the subsistence fishery. Attractive aquarium species.

Red barb *Enteromius fasciolatus* (Günther, 1868)
Masaradina (B)

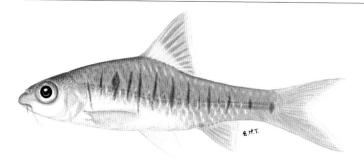

SL: 60 mm; D iii, 8; A iii, 5. 25–30 scales in lateral line, 12 scales around the caudal peduncle. Body slender with a terminal mouth. Two pairs of barbels. Colour olive to rose or red, silvery below, with 10–15 vertical black bars, the last forming a spot on the caudal peduncle. This is the only barb in the area with vertical bars. Black spot on anal fin origin. Fins translucent rose. Males smaller and more slender than females.

These colourful barbs are common on the margins of streams and rivers but are uncommon on shallow floodplains. Prefer shallow, well-oxygenated, papyrus-fringed edges of streams and river channels, and the edges of perennial lagoons and marshes. Not found in open water. They are most active at dawn and dusk, when they feed on small insects, worms, crustaceans and algae attached to plants, and shelter under the cover of plants at midday. They migrate onto floodplains to spawn during summer, laying their eggs among plants. As in most barbs, they have an extended spawning season – from September to March – in the northern delta, but only spawn between September and December in the southern seasonal swamp. Distributed throughout the Okavango Delta and Kavango and Chobe systems. Elsewhere they are found in the Cunene, upper and middle Zambezi, Kafue and Congo systems and in the Bangweulu swamps. Commonly caught by traditional fishermen. An attractive aquarium species. First collected in Angola in the 1860s by the Austrian explorer Friedrich Welwitsch, after whom the desert plant *Welwitschia mirabilis* ('tumbo') is named.

Sickle-fin barb *Enteromius haasianus* (David, 1936)
Masaradina (B)

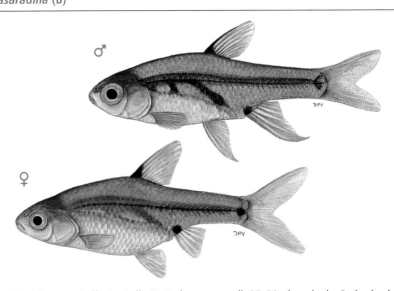

SL: 32 mm; D ii, 8; A ii, 5. Scales very small, 35–38 along body. Body slender, small. Mouth terminal, no barbels. No lateral line. Eyes very large. Live fishes are almost transparent underwater. Body translucent silvery brown, changing to rosy red in breeding males. In mature males, the anal fin is sickle-shaped and the pelvic fins are elongated; these fins are tinged orange-pink during summer. Thin line along body ends in a spot at the base of the tail; spots also on the bases of the dorsal and anal fins.

A small barb that is abundant on the edges of shallow, well-vegetated floodplains and slow-flowing rivers, and in well-vegetated backwater lagoons, but is absent from fast-flowing waters. Tolerant of extreme environmental conditions and one of the last species found as floodplain pools dry out. Feeds on small insects and algae on plant stems. Migrates onto floodplains to spawn during the summer flood, laying eggs amongst plants. Distributed throughout the Okavango Delta and Chobe River. Elsewhere they are found in the Cunene, Zambezi, Kafue, Pungwe and Zambian Congo systems and in Lake Bangweulu. Caught in traps by subsistence fishermen. An attractive aquarium species.

Redspot barb *Enteromius kerstenii* (Peters, 1868)
Masaradina (B)

SL: 75 mm; D III, 7; A iii, 5. 23–27 scales in lateral line, 12 scales around the caudal peduncle. Deep bodied, mouth terminal, two pairs of barbels. Upper body light olive-silver, silvery below. Distinctive red, orange or yellow spot on the gill cover (hence the common name). Black zigzag pattern along the midbody, and chevrons along the lateral line. Tail fin forked. Last unbranched ray of the dorsal fin stiff and serrated.

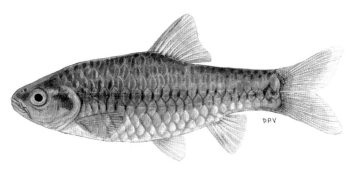

A shoaling species found in sheltered, well-vegetated habitats, also rocky substrates bordering large rivers and channels in the panhandle, and in the Kavango (Namibia) and Cubango (Angola) rivers. Prefers clear, well-oxygenated habitats where it feeds on insects, snails, plants, seeds and algae. Migrates upstream during the rainy season, after the arrival of the annual floodwaters, and moves onto recently inundated floodplains to lay its eggs on grasses and aquatic vegetation. Not recorded from the seasonal swamp or the Chobe River. Elsewhere these barbs are found in lakes Victoria, Tanganyika and Kivu, in the Congo, Cunene, upper and lower Zambezi and Kafue systems, and in east coast rivers in Kenya, Tanzania and Mozambique. Their abundance may be reduced by increased water turbidity arising from agriculture. A minor component of the subsistence fishery.

Line-spotted barb *Enteromius lineomaculatus* (Boulenger, 1903)
Masaradina, Msindi (B)

SL: 86 mm; D iii, 8; A iii, 5. 26–32 scales in the lateral line, 12 scales around the caudal peduncle. Body elongate, eye large. Mouth terminal, with two pairs of long barbels. Last unbranched ray of the dorsal fin flexible and unserrated. Body colour silver, yellow or translucent brown above, silvery below, with a series of 4–7 black spots forming a black band above the lateral line. Dark chevron markings form a broken line along the lateral line. Males bright gold when breeding.

The line-spotted barb inhabits small streams and large river channels as well as shallow marginal swamps. Feeds on insects, snails, plants, seeds and algae. Moves upstream to spawn in recently inundated grassy areas. In the region known only from the Kavango (Namibia) and Cubango (Angola) rivers. It has not, as yet, been recorded from the

Okavango Delta or Chobe River, although it may occur in the riverine panhandle. Elsewhere they are found throughout central and East Africa, in the Cunene, upper Zambezi, upper Congo, Buzi and Limpopo rivers, and in upland streams north of Lake Malawi. A small component of the subsistence fishery.

Copperstripe barb *Enteromius multilineatus* (Worthington, 1933)
Masaradina (B)

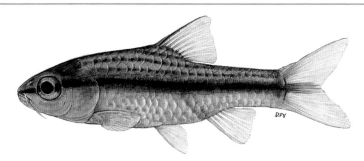

SL: 45 mm; D III, 7–8; A iii, 5. 25–27 scales in lateral line, 12 scales around the caudal peduncle. Body short, mouth terminal, two pairs of barbels. First dorsal spine serrated, enlarged scales at base of dorsal fin. Colour translucent, olive-grey-brown above with distinct coppery stripe from snout to tail in the males. Also, shadow stripes run along the back and a middle stripe runs from the snout through the eye, along the body and onto the tail fin. Silvery-brown below. Fins orange to red in juveniles, yellow to deep orange in adults.

A small, brightly coloured barb that is common on the margins of well-oxygenated, slow-flowing rivers, in grassy floodplains and in well-vegetated backwater lagoons, preferring dense plant cover. Often hides under floating plants or grass mats near the water surface. Feeds on algae and small invertebrates living on plants. Breeds between October and March, after rain or after the flood, depositing its eggs on submerged plants. Found mainly in the perennial upper reaches of the Okavango Delta, upstream in the Kavango River in Namibia and the Cubango River in Angola, as well as in the Chobe River. Elsewhere known from the Cunene, upper and middle Zambezi, Kafue and upper Congo systems and from Lake Bangweulu. Caught by subsistence fishermen using traditional traps and baskets. Despite its striking and attractive appearance it was only described in 1933.

Straightfin barb   *Enteromius paludinosus* (Peters, 1852)
Masaradina, Msindi (B)

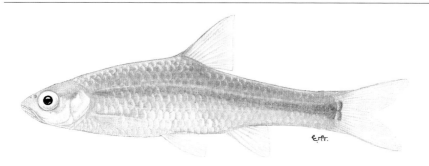

SL: 150mm; D III, 7; A iii, 5. 32–36 scales in lateral line, 16 scales around the caudal peduncle, both scale counts being more than those for other barbs. Body slender, head pointed, mouth small, terminal, with two pairs of short barbels. First dorsal fin ray serrated. Rear margin of dorsal fin perpendicular to horizontal when erect, dorsal fin origin behind pelvic fin origin. Body light olive-brown above, silvery below. Fins light olive to transparent. Body lighter silvery grey in turbid waters, darker in clear water. In large (and dead) specimens a faint lateral stripe is visible. Females larger than males.

Probably the most abundant fish in the Okavango Delta and Chobe River. Inhabits quiet, well-vegetated waters in slow-flowing channels, floodplains and backwater lagoons. Hardy and tolerant of extreme environmental conditions. In December 1982 this barb and the sharptooth catfish were the last fish species remaining in isolated pools on the Kunyere River near Toteng village during a drought. Omnivorous, feeding on a wide variety of aquatic insects, crustaceans and small snails as well as on algae, diatoms, detritus, aquatic plants and planktonic copepods. It is an important prey species of sharptooth catfish, largemouth breams and fish-eating birds.

Its survival strategy includes breeding early and laying many eggs. The females lay 250–800 eggs at the age of one year and 50–60 mm SL, and up to 2,500 eggs at 112 mm. Spawning takes place during the summer rainy season and after the arrival of the annual flood in the perennial upper delta.

Carries out upstream migrations and lateral movements onto recently inundated floodplains to lay its eggs on the new growth of grasses and aquatic plants. In the seasonal southern delta it spawns along the margins of the Boro, Thamalakane and Boteti rivers and on the floodplains. Widespread in East Africa, extending southwards to KwaZulu-Natal, and westwards to the Orange River. Caught by subsistence fishermen using traditional fishing baskets and traps as well as small-mesh gill nets (24–30 mm stretched mesh). The straightfin barb is an important component of the *matemba* fishery on Lake Chilwa in Malawi, where it is caught using nets and traps and then sun-dried. The specific name *paludinosus* refers to its preference for swampy habitats, whereas the common name 'straightfin' refers to the vertical hind margin of the erect dorsal fin.

Dashtail barb   *Enteromius poechii* (Steindachner, 1911)
Masaradina (B)

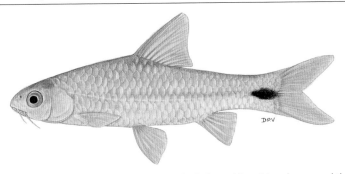

SL: 110 mm; D III, 8; A iii, 5. 31–33 scales in lateral line, 14 scales around the caudal peduncle. Scales have radiate lines. Body robust, two pairs of barbels. Dorsal fin with simple spine. Silvery olive-brown above, silver below, with prominent oblong black dot at base of tail fin.

A common, fairly large shoaling barb that inhabits slower-flowing river channels, floodplains and well-vegetated backwater lagoons. It is frequently found with the striped robber, which it strongly resembles, suggesting that there may be mimicry between them. Feeds on insects and other small organisms. Migrates upstream to breed in slower-flowing river channels and inundated floodplains during summer, laying eggs among submerged plants. Common throughout the Okavango Delta and Chobe River. Elsewhere found in the Kavango, Cunene and upper Zambezi systems. Caught by traditional fishermen using fishing baskets, weirs, handmade hooks and lines and small-mesh gill nets (24–30 mm stretched mesh), in open waters in river channels and lagoons. Protected in the Moremi Game Reserve and Chobe National Park. Suitable bait for tigerfish. Named after Dr W. Pöch who collected the first specimens from the Okavango Delta in 1909.

Beira barb   *Enteromius radiatus* (Peters, 1853)
Masaradina (B)

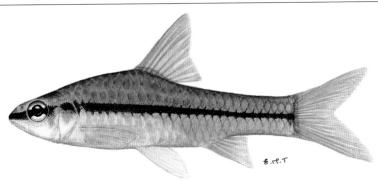

SL: 120 mm; D iii, 8; A iii, 5. 24–29 scales in lateral line, 12 scales around the caudal peduncle. Body slender with a small terminal mouth; two pairs of very short barbels. Upper body olive to silver, belly silvery white, fins tinted salmon or orange with grey edges. Red portion of eye conspicuous. A dark lateral stripe extends straight from the snout to the tail. The centres of the scales above the lateral stripe are dotted, giving the impression of faint stripes. Lines of minute pores on the sides and top of the head are distinctive.

A common, widely distributed barb that inhabits the shallow, vegetated reaches of slow-flowing channels, sawgrass marshes and backwater lagoons. Active at night, feeding on aquatic invertebrates. Migrates onto the floodplains to spawn during the annual flood between September and March. Distributed throughout the Okavango Delta and Chobe and Zambezi systems. Elsewhere it is found in the Congo and Cunene systems and in east coast rivers as far south as the Phongolo. Caught by traditional fishermen in traps laid in channels and on floodplains. An attractive aquarium species. Named by the German naturalist Wilhelm Peters, after its radiately striated scales, a feature shared by all small barbs.

Thamalakane barb   *Enteromius thamalakanensis* (Fowler, 1935)
Masaradina (B)

TL: 40 mm; D iii, 8; A iii, 5. 25–29 scales in lateral line, 12 around the caudal peduncle. A small barb with a slender body. Two pairs of long barbels. Thin black lateral stripe extends from the snout to the tail, sometimes with a distinct tail spot. Light brown above, silvery white on sides and below. Breeding male golden.

A common barb that inhabits the well-vegetated margins of rivers and lagoons, floodplain pools and backwaters. Feeds on insects and algae attached to submerged plants (periphyton). Breeds in summer among riverside vegetation and on floodplains, laying its eggs on submerged vegetation. Common throughout the Okavango Delta and abundant in the lower seasonal swamp and in the Boro, Boteti and Thamalakane rivers. Also inhabits perennially flooded lagoons such as Dungu and Xakanaxa and the Maqwexana Pools. Restricted to the Okavango Delta and the Kavango, Chobe and upper Zambezi systems. Regularly caught by subsistence fishermen. An attractive aquarium species. Named by H.W. Fowler after the Thamalakane River at Maun, where it was first discovered in 1935.

Longbeard barb *Enteromius unitaeniatus* (Günther, 1866)
Masaradina (B)

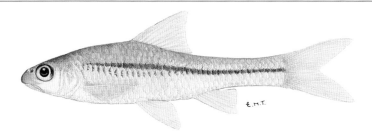

SL: 140 mm; D iii, 8; A iii, 5–6. Body elongate with inferior mouth. Scales 29–35 in lateral line, two pairs of long barbels. Eyes large. Translucent brown on upper body, silvery-white below, with prominent dark lateral stripe and chevron markings on lateral line.

A widespread species found in a variety of habitats including fast- and slow-flowing river channels with sandy substrates, sandy back eddies bordering rapids, and well-vegetated perennial lagoons, such as Xakanaxa, Gadikwe and Xobecqa. Does not normally occur in floodplains or backwater lagoons. Feeds on benthic invertebrates, plants and grass seeds. Breeds immediately after the summer rains, among aquatic vegetation. Distributed throughout the Okavango Delta and Chobe River. Elsewhere found in the Zambian Congo, Cunene and upper Zambezi systems south to the Phongolo River, but absent from the lower Zambezi, Pungwe and Buzi rivers. Protected in the Moremi Game Reserve and Chobe National Park. Caught in the subsistence fishery using woven baskets and small-mesh gill nets (24–30 mm stretched mesh).

Northern barred minnow *Opsaridium zambezense* (Peters, 1852)
Masaradina (B)

SL: 120 mm; D iii, 8–10; A iii, 11–13. Body slender with 12 paired vertical bars, often turquoise in colour. Scales 40–44 in lateral line, 14 around the caudal peduncle. Low lateral line curves down towards the ventral surface of the body. Dorsal fin rounded, anal fin concave, tail fin deeply forked, mouth large, lacks barbels. Silvery olive to yellow-green, mature males pink-red on body and fins.

A shoaling species found in shallow water flowing over sand or gravel, often along river banks and especially in the upstream reaches of pools below rapids or runs. Also found under floating papyrus islands that detach during the flood. Feeds on bottom-living invertebrates and shrimps as well as adult insects taken at the water surface. Breeds in spring and summer. Found in flowing channels of the middle and upper Okavango Delta, the Kavango and Zambezi as well as the Pungwe rivers; absent from the Kafue and Cunene rivers and not known from the Chobe River. Its very specific habitat preferences suggest that its presence may be a sensitive indicator of environmental stability. Caught in the subsistence fishery using woven baskets and traps and by young boys with a simple handmade hook and line, using worm bait.

CITHARINES   Distichodontidae

A family of fishes confined to Africa. Its members have square jaws with two rows of teeth, distinctive ctenoid scales, and many have conspicuous bars on the body. Anal fin with less than 16 branched rays, tail fin forked, adipose fin usually present. Their closest relatives in Africa are the Hepsetidae (African pikes) and Alestidae (tigerfish and robbers). Four species known from the area.

Dwarf citharine   *Nannocharax machadoi* (Poll, 1967)

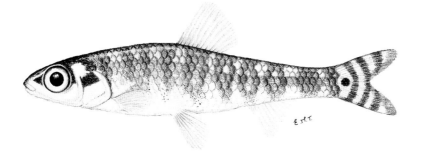

SL: 40 mm; D iii, 10–11; A iii, 8. 34–36 ctenoid scales in lateral line, 12 around the caudal peduncle. Lateral line restricted to 8–9 scales behind the head. Body slender, mouth terminal, on a pointed snout. Eyes very large. Fins short, tail fin with a prominent dark eye-spot and 2–3 curved bands, other fins light grey. No adipose fin. Translucent, light olive above, silvery below, with 12–16 irregular bars along the body. Breeding males darker.

A small citharine that inhabits the dense papyrus and reed stands that line the mainstream fringes and tributary channels of permanent rivers. Also found in well-vegetated perennial lagoons. Feeds by picking periphyton (minute, attached algae and diatoms) and tiny invertebrates from the stems and leaves of water plants. Spawns during the summer rainy season and after the arrival of the annual floodwaters. Found in the perennial upper reaches of the Okavango Delta but not in the seasonal southern reaches. Also occurs in the Kavango River in Namibia and in the Chobe River. Elsewhere it is found in the upper and middle Zambezi, Kafue and Cunene systems. Its southern limit of distribution is the Okavango Delta. Attractive aquarium species.

Broadbar citharine *Nannocharax macropterus* Pellegrin, 1926

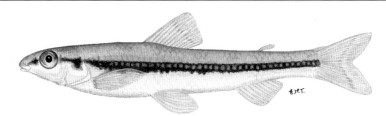

SL: 60 mm; D iii, 9–11; A ii, 8. 40–42 ctenoid scales in lateral line, 12 around the caudal peduncle. Body slender, mouth terminal, eyes large, adipose fin present. Lateral line complete. Pectoral fins long, reaching the pelvics. Translucent light olive above, white below, with a series of broad lateral bars often fused into a dark lateral band.

A flowing-water (rheophilic) species found among the roots of floating papyrus, under reed mats and in aquatic plant beds in the riverine panhandle. Absent from floodplains and backwater lagoons in the perennial delta and also not known from the seasonal delta. Feeds on small invertebrates and periphyton from the stems and roots of plants. Makes seasonal migrations during the summer rainy season and after the arrival of the annual flood to spawn. Absent from the Chobe River. Elsewhere it inhabits moderate- to fast-flowing river channels in the upper Zambezi, Kafue and Kasai Congo systems. Protected in the Moremi Game Reserve. Its southern limit of distribution is the Okavango Delta.

Multibar citharine *Nannocharax multifasciatus* (Boulenger, 1923)

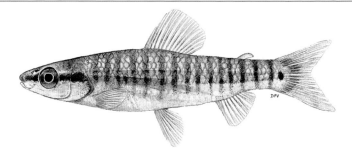

SL: 45 mm; D iii, 10–12; A iii, 8–9. 40–44 ctenoid scales in lateral line, lateral line incomplete, 16 around the caudal peduncle. Body slender, compressed. Head pointed, mouth terminal, eyes large. Fins short. Adipose fin present. Translucent light olive above with dark edges to the scales, 16–25 dark vertical bars along body, silvery-yellow below. Tail fin with prominent spot and one dark curved band.

A small midwater species that inhabits the flowing vegetated margins of rivers and lagoons in the riverine panhandle, oxbow lagoons and northern perennial swamp, but not the seasonal swamp. Picks small invertebrates from the stems and rootballs of plants. Does not form shoals. Makes seasonal movements onto the floodplains during the summer rainy season, and after the arrival of the annual flood, to spawn. Elsewhere it is found in the upper Zambezi, Cunene, Kafue and Zambian Congo systems. Its southern limit of distribution is the Okavango Delta. The scientific name means 'a dwarf fish with many vertical bars'. First collected in the upper Zambezi River by Reverend L. Jalla, and one of the last fish species to be named by the legendary biologist George Boulenger, who described over 2,000 new fish, amphibian and reptile species, as well as many plants.

ROBBERS AND TIGERFISH   Alestidae

A large family of African freshwater fishes that includes many familiar species. They are often predators and have sharp teeth on their jaws. Dorsal fin behind pelvic fins, adipose fin present, tail fin forked. Head ovoid, cheeks with bony plates. Scales usually large. Lateral line dips low on body. Four species known from the area.

Striped robber   *Brycinus lateralis* (Boulenger, 1900)
Nchenga (B)

SL: 140 mm; D ii, 8; A iii, 15–16. 30–33 scales in lateral line, 10–14 (usually 12) scales around the caudal peduncle. Mouth terminal, with sharp, multicuspid teeth. Eyes large, yellow. Colour silvery, brown or bluish above, with a faint yellow lateral band, which ends in a large black dash, outlined with yellow, at the base of the tail fin. The lateral band darkens in large or dead specimens. Leading rays of the anal fin extended in males. Adipose fin yellow, other fins transparent with yellowish tinge along their bases. Females larger than males.

An abundant midwater shoaling species with a wide distribution. Inhabits the slower-flowing, well-vegetated edges of smaller river channels, such as the Boro, Thamalakane and Boteti, as well as open-water lagoons in the perennial swamp, such as Xakanaxa, Gadikwe and Xobecqa. Its range is probably restricted by predatory tigerfish. An active predator that feeds on small aquatic animals as well as terrestrial insects that fall on the water surface; sometimes feeds on plant material. Preyed on by tigerfish, southern African pike, other predatory fish, fish-eating birds and crocodiles. Often found together with dashtail and threespot barbs, which it resembles, suggesting mimicry.

Forms shoals, which migrate upstream to spawn in recently inundated floodplains and backwater channels after rain and the annual flood. Breeds from September to February. Large females produce over 12,000 eggs.

Found throughout the Okavango Delta and Chobe River. Also in the Kavango, Cunene, Luapala Congo, upper Zambezi and Kafue systems and in east coast rivers and swamps as far south as the St Lucia wetland in KwaZulu-Natal. Frequently caught in subsistence and commercial fisheries. Anglers catch it with very small hooks and worms, or slices of fish or red meat. Excellent live bait for tigerfish, southern African pike or largemouth bream.

Tigerfish   *Hydrocynus vittatus*   Castelnau, 1861
Ndweshi (B), *Ngwesi* (B), *Ngweshe* (S), *Ngwethi* (H)

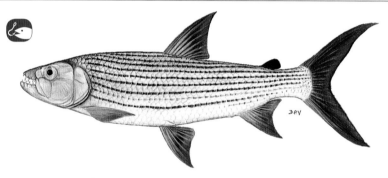

FL: ♂ 500 mm; ♀ 700 mm; D ii, 7–8; A iii, 10–13. 43–48 scales in lateral line, 15–16 around the caudal peduncle. Body streamlined, fusiform. Silvery above, with a bluish sheen on the back and a series of thin black stripes running horizontally, hence its scientific name, which means 'striped waterdog'. The young are silver until they reach a length of 20 mm, and full adult colours develop when they reach 100 mm. Head large, with bony cheeks and powerful jaws, each with a set of eight large, protruding, sharp, pointed teeth. Eyes protected by a vertical transparent eyelid. Adipose fin black, tail fin deeply forked, yellow to blood red, with a black edge. Tip and trailing edge of dorsal fin black. Angling record in Zimbabwe is 15.507 kg, but most large specimens weigh 5–7 kg.

An iconic African freshwater fish that is one of the greatest sporting fish in the world. A voracious predator, with formidable teeth that are used to grasp and tear prey. It inhabits warm, well-oxygenated water in the riverine panhandle, larger channels and northern perennial lagoons, such as Xakanaxa, Gadikwe and Xobecqa, but has limited environmental tolerance and does not inhabit seasonal environments. Common in the Chobe River. Tigerfish form packs of similarly sized fish that can attack and kill any other fish in the Okavango Delta. Pack hunting has been observed near Ngarange

Angler with a fine tigerfish

village and elsewhere in the riverine panhandle and perennial swamp. Unlike catfish 'pack hunters', which swarm upstream in dense shoals, tigerfish carry out a form of social hunting whereby they patrol channel mouths when the floodwaters are receding and catch fish that are migrating from the seasonal floodplains into perennial river channels. During hunting forays they sometimes bite chunks of flesh from large prey fish, as do piranhas, their relatives in South America.

Tigerfish dominate aquatic communities in open waters and outcompete all other predatory fish, such as southern African pike and largemouth bream, which tend to hunt in side channels, floodplains and backwater lagoons. During the day tigerfish swim close to the water surface, but they hunt in deeper water at dawn and dusk. Where tigerfish are absent, such as in the seasonal southern waterways and lagoons of the Okavango Delta, pike and largemouth bream occupy the niche of top open-water predators. Tigerfish feed mainly on fish, especially slender-bodied shoaling species, and are able to catch prey up to 40% of their length. They are cannibalistic, so they always swim in similar-sized shoals. Tigerfish have also been known to eat snakes and small mammals. Whole sets of teeth are regularly replaced throughout their lives, with the new teeth developing in the jaws, below the functional teeth. Juveniles feed on insects and zooplankton. Predators include larger tigerfish and fish eagles.

In the Okavango Delta, spawning takes place between October and November, prior to the arrival of the rains and annual floodwaters, when fish migrate both upstream and downstream to find suitable spawning sites. Males reach sexual maturity at 2–3 years of age and 300–400 mm FL, whereas females usually mature at lengths greater than 400 mm. Spawning may take place at night. Fecundity is very high, with the largest females (650–700 mm FL) producing over 780,000 eggs, of which over 150,000 may be released at a time. The eggs are deposited on the stems of papyrus, reeds and other submerged plants.

Newly hatched tigerfish fry often inhabit areas that have been cleaned out by the tens of thousands of catfish that participate in the annual catfish run. When the tigerfish are very small, they hide and feed in or near papyrus rootballs. When the annual floodwaters reach the panhandle (usually by mid-January), the current and some active swimming help them to reach the floodplains, where they feed and grow to 120–140 mm FL. When they reach lengths of 150–160 mm FL, they are large enough to hunt in the mainstream channels. They grow rapidly, reaching 160–200 mm FL by one year and 300 mm FL after two years. Males mature earlier, and generally die younger, than females, so most tigerfish larger than 600 mm are female.

Elsewhere they are found in the Kavango, Zambezi and Limpopo systems and the lowland reaches of east coast rivers as far south as the Phongolo River.

Tigerfish are highly prized in sports fishing for their lively fighting ability, although they often fight their way off the hook, which may not always lodge in their bony mouths. They are caught from the shore or from boats using baited hooks, spoons, spinners or flies, and mid-sized specimens (about 4 kg) are considered to be the best fighters. Annual sport-fishing competitions have been organized in the Okavango Delta and Chobe River that attract sport fishermen from many countries. Tigerfish are also caught in commercial and subsistence fisheries. The flesh spoils easily and is not as tasty as that of cichlids, but pickled or smoked tigerfish is regarded as a delicacy.

The abundance of tigerfish has declined in some areas because of water pollution caused by the increased use of fertilizers upstream in Namibia, overfishing using gill nets, the damage caused by cattle that trample floodplain habitats, and fires that are intentionally lit to clear areas for grazing. Considering the economic importance of tigerfish, it is essential that these impacts are brought under control. The tigerfish can be bred in captivity with difficulty, but it cannot be considered an aquaculture species. F. Daviaud collected the type specimen (from which the species was first described) from Lake Ngami in 1858. The largest tigerfish species from the Congo River, *Hydrocynus goliath*, reaches over 45 kg.

Silver robber   *Micralestes acutidens* (Peters, 1852)
Misindi (B), *Oxhwara* (B), *Manxhee* (H)

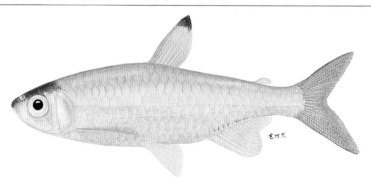

SL: 80 mm; D ii, 8; A iii, 14–16. 23–28 scales in lateral line. Body slender, fusiform, eyes large, mouth terminal, jaws with sharp multicuspid teeth. Has a distinctive black tip on the dorsal fin. Body silvery, often with a greenish tinge. Fins pale yellow or orange, with blackish fringe, front rays of anal fin in males extended. Females grow larger than males.

A small, abundant, midwater- to surface-swimming predator that is distributed throughout the riverine panhandle and perennial swamp, and is also common in lagoons, such as Xakanaxa, Gadikwe and Xobecqa. It has not been recorded from the seasonal delta but is found in the Chobe River. Forms shoals in clear, flowing or standing open water lined with papyrus and reed beds. Feeds on insect larvae, shrimps, fish eggs and fry, winged insects, zooplankton and seeds. Co-exists with tigerfish in permanent waterways, although it is heavily preyed on by that apex predator. Reaches sexual maturity after one year, lives for about three years. Breeding shoals migrate upstream after the first summer rains and with the rising floodwaters, and breeding takes place throughout the summer rainy season. Females produce about 700 eggs per spawning and place the adhesive eggs on plant stems.

Elsewhere occurs in the Cunene, Kavango, Zambezi and Congo systems and in east coast rivers as far south as the Phongolo.

Caught in traditional fish traps, set in reed weirs on floodplains when the water is receding. Used as bait for tigerfish and southern African pike, and often strips bait from anglers' hooks. Aggressive aquarium fish. The scientific name means 'small robber with sharp teeth'. First collected in the lower Zambezi system in the 1840s, by the German scientist Wilhelm Peters.

Slender robber   *Rhabdalestes maunensis* (Fowler, 1935)

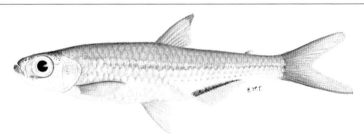

SL: 60 mm; D ii, 7–9; A iii, 16–19. 33–36 cycloid scales in lateral line. Body more slender than in other robbers. Head small, eye large, mouth terminal and slightly upturned. Yellow to light brown above, with an iridescent bluish band along the body, black band along the base of the anal fin and silvery-white head and belly. Fins pointed, leading rays of anal fin elongated in males. Adipose fin yellow, tail fin yellow with black edge.

A shoaling midwater species that inhabits the fringes of dense papyrus and reed mats, adjacent to mainstream channels and coves in the Okavango Delta and the Kavango and Chobe rivers. Also inhabits seasonal, vegetated floodplain habitats. Feeds on small aquatic insects and their larvae and other invertebrates. Spawns during the summer rainy season or after the annual flood in newly inundated floodplains and backwater channels. Most commonly found in the riverine panhandle and northern perennial swamp and lagoons, as well as in the southern seasonal swamp at Nxaragha Lagoon on the lower Boro River, and in Chanogha Lagoon on the Boteti River. Also found in the Chobe River. Elsewhere occurs in the upper Zambezi, Cunene and Kafue systems. Named after the town Maun, where it was first collected. An attractive aquarium species.

AFRICAN PIKES Hepsetidae

A uniquely African freshwater fish family, with six species. Widespread throughout the western parts of south, central and west Africa and easily recognized by their sharply pointed head, crocodile-like jaws and distinctive coloration. Dorsal fin behind pelvic fins, adipose fin present, tail fin forked. Cheeks with bony plates. Scales moderate. One species known from the region.

Southern African pike *Hepsetus cuvieri* (Castelnau, 1861)
Nero (S), *Nyeru* (S), *Nyiro* (H), *Onyiro* (B), *Molumezi* (Chobe area)

FL: 470 mm; D ii, 7; A ii, 9. 48–55 small cycloid scales in lateral line, 24 around the caudal peduncle. Body torpedo-shaped, head pointed, mouth large. Jaws with prominent, unevenly protruding, sharp canine teeth. In adults, both jaws have pairs of skin flaps. Dorsal and anal fins set far back on the body, tail fin forked, lobe-like adipose fin present. Brassy olive with dark brown blotches above, cream below. Fins with black spots, adipose fin orange with black spots. Head brownish-green with 3–4 dark stripes radiating out from the eye. Reaches about 2 kg, with females growing larger than males. Previously known as *Hepsetus odoe*.

An easily recognizable predator, with a pointed head, crocodile-like jaws and distinctive brown-spotted coloration. It occurs in a wide variety of habitats, from the slow-flowing reaches of rivers and tributaries to deep lagoons and channels through the swamps, but always on the sheltered fringes. It rarely ventures into open water due to competition from tigerfish. In Nxaragha and Qorokwe lagoons, these pike have been caught at dusk and dawn in open water using gill nets, but they have not been caught in mainstream channels.

In contrast with the tigerfish, which is a fast-swimming, marauding predator, the pike is an ambush predator. Pike are very well camouflaged in dappled shallow water and launch their attacks from the shelter of reed stems, both during the day and at night. Juveniles prey on small invertebrates and small fish, whereas adults prey exclusively on fish, especially cichlids, barbs, topminnows and robbers. They grow rapidly and reach sexual maturity after two years, at a length of about 200 mm in males and 250 mm in females. They are relatively short-lived with a life span of 4–5 years. Their predators include tigerfish, large catfish and fish-eating birds.

Spawning begins in September and continues until February, with each female spawning several times. Adult fish form pairs and build foam nests that float on the water surface, similar to those of some frogs, among the vertical stems of emergent aquatic plants on the sheltered fringes of lagoons, oxbow lakes and backwaters. As the water level rises and falls, the nests 'ride' up and down the plant stems, thus maintaining their position on the water surface. Females produce relatively few (about 8,000) eggs per season. The eggs are fairly large and provide a generous amount of yolk for the developing embryos to feed on.

The fertilized eggs are deposited in the foam nest and are guarded by both parents, which lurk nearby and aggressively chase away predators. When they hatch, the fry move through the foam to the base of the nest, where they attach themselves using a cement gland on their heads and hang into the water. While attached to the nest they may obtain nutrients from their yolk sacs, as well as from organic matter trapped in the foam nest. As the fry develop into juveniles they become less reliant on the shelter provided by the nest and, after about one week, become free swimming and feed independently on detritus and small aquatic animals.

The African pike family is uniquely African. Southern African pike are distributed throughout the Okavango Delta and Chobe River, though they are more common in the southern seasonal delta, where tigerfish are uncommon. Elsewhere they occur in the Cunene, Kavango, upper Zambezi, Kafue and southern tributaries of the Congo systems, but they are absent from the Zambian Congo system. They were not recorded from the middle Zambezi River before Lake Kariba was created, but they have been recorded from Lake Kariba since 1989. Their southern limit of distribution is the Okavango Delta.

Southern African pike are frequently caught in subsistence and commercial

K. Holden

Southern African pike fry forming a star shape by adhering to one another using the cement glands on their heads

fisheries in the Kavango and Chobe systems. They are excellent sport fish on light tackle and can be caught on small, three-hooked silver spinners or using barbs or topminnows as live bait. Bass plugs, flies or hooks baited with earthworms or grasshoppers are also used to catch pike. As the pike's teeth do not interlock like those of the tigerfish, a steel trace is advisable, but not essential. Like the tigerfish, pike leap out of the water when hooked.

Small catfishes found only in Africa. They prefer clear, running streams. They have three pairs of simple barbels and two dorsal fins, the first short with rays, the hind fin fleshy. Mountain catfish (*Amphilius* spp.) have a filamentous leading pectoral fin ray, whereas sand catlets (*Zaireichthys* spp.) have short, barbed spines in the dorsal or pectoral fins, a short anal fin and a tail fin that is either truncate or rounded. Pectoral fins low on body, pelvic fins far back. Swim bladder reduced and partly encapsulated. Four species known from the region. Sand catlets were previously placed in the family Bagridae.

Stargazer mountain catfish *Amphilius uranoscopus* (Pfeffer, 1889)
Nxhaoxhaa (B)

TL: 170 mm; D i, 6; A iii, 5–7. Body and head compressed, eyes small and on top of head. First dorsal fin short, with a soft simple ray, adipose fin short and deep, notched behind. Caudal peduncle length equal to its depth, caudal fin emarginate or shallowly forked. Fan-like pectoral and pelvic fins lack spines. Colour variable, usually yellowish-brown or greyish-brown, mottled or with black shadows, blotches or spots.

A small, bottom-dwelling predator that prefers clear, flowing water in rocky riffles and under waterfalls. Feeds on aquatic insects and other small organisms taken from rock surfaces. Breeds in summer, laying its eggs under stones. The juveniles closely resemble tadpoles in body shape and swimming action. Preyed on by largemouth bream and southern African pike. Distribution limited to the riverine panhandle and Kavango and Cubango systems in Namibia and Angola. Not recorded in the Okavango Delta or Chobe River, although it may occur there. Elsewhere found in the Zambezi system, throughout central Africa and in east coast rivers south to the Mkuze system in KwaZulu-Natal. The species name *uranoscopus* and common name 'stargazer' refer to the upturned eyes on top of the head.

Blotched sand catlet   *Zaireichthys conspicuus* Eccles, Tweddle & Skelton, 2011

P. Skelton (NGOWP)

SL: 35 mm; D II, 6 ; A iii–iv, 6–7. Body depressed, head large and rounded with fleshy lips, nostrils widely separated. Three pairs of short, simple barbels. Lateral line short. Two dorsal fins, the first short, with a short spine. Adipose fin large, extending to behind anal fin. Pectoral fins with barbed spine, caudal fin truncate. Skin on dorsal surface of head and body with minute papillae. Background colour beige, with faint orange tint in adipose and upper tail fin. Head brownish, with yellow cheeks. Body with dark brown or black patches that often join, forming a reticulated pattern or broad vertical stripes.

A very small, robust species found over sandy substrates in flowing waters. Produces copious amounts of slime when handled. Feeds on small invertebrates, such as mayfly nymphs and caddis fly larvae. Breeds in summer. A Zambezi species that is also found in the Chobe, Kavango and Cubango systems. The specific name refers to its bold markings.

Kavango sand catlet   *Zaireichthys kavangoensis* Eccles, Tweddle & Skelton, 2011
Dimbotu (H)

P. Skelton (NGOWP)

SL: 27 mm; D II, 5; A iv–vi, 5–6. Body depressed. Head large and rounded, eyes relatively large. Mouth inferior, with fleshy lips, three pairs of moderately sized, simple barbels, nostrils widely separated. Fins small, with barbed spines, first dorsal fin short, spine short and simple, adipose fin long and low, pectoral spines with barbs on hind edge. Colour off-white with a series of finely speckled dark patches on the upper body and sides.

A very small catlet that is found on sandy substrates in flowing waters and on the edges of rocky rapids. Wriggles into the sand to hide, with only the eyes protruding. Produces copious amounts of slime when handled. Feeds on small invertebrates in the drift, especially mayfly nymphs and caddis fly larvae. Breeds in summer. Only known from the Kavango River above Popa Rapids in Namibia and Angola and not as yet recorded from the Okavango Delta or Chobe River, although it may occur there. A newly described species of sand catlet.

Pallid sand catlet
Zaireichthys pallidus Eccles, Tweddle & Skelton, 2011
Dimbotu (H)

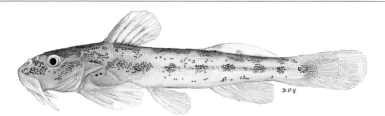

SL: 25 mm; D II, 4–5; A iv–vii, 5–6. Body small, slender and compressed, head depressed and blunt in front. Mouth inferior, three pairs of relatively long, simple barbels, nostrils widely spaced, eyes moderately sized. Small tooth patch on upper jaw. Two dorsal fins, the first short with a simple spine, adipose fin long and low. Pectoral fins with barbed spine, fan shaped. Tail fin sub-truncate. Body pale creamy-white, with a series of faint dark blotches (usually nine) along the sides, and traces of additional series above and below.

Paler and less conspicuously marked than other sand catlets. Occurs in shallow water over sandy substrates and hides in the sand with only its eyes protruding. Feeds on detritus, algae, seeds and aquatic insect larvae. Only found in the Kwando and Chobe rivers and not known from the Okavango Delta. Elsewhere occurs in the upper Zambezi river system as far upstream as the Barotse floodplain in Zambia. This species may represent a complex of several different species, and further taxonomic study is needed.

P. Skelton (NGOWP)

Pallid sand catlets favour sandy riffle habitat.

Common and familiar catfishes with a bony, flattened head, elongate body and long dorsal and anal fins. Pectoral fins high on body, pelvic fins far back. No spine in the dorsal fin, strong spines in the pectoral fins, tail fin rounded. Four pairs of barbels, often long. Small eyes. Usually grey or brown but may be mottled. These are hardy fishes that can breathe air and survive desiccation using air-breathing organs located in chambers above their gills. Some species attain a large size, but others are small. Mostly nocturnal and crepuscular (active at dawn and dusk). Six species known from the region.

Sharptooth catfish   *Clarias gariepinus* (Burchell, 1822)
Onyanda (B), *Dituni* (S), *Duni* (S), *Thikokoro* (H), *Ndombi* (Chobe area)

SL: 1.4 m; D 61–75; A, 45–65. Body elongate and strongly compressed towards the tail, with a large, flattened, bony head. Mouth broad, terminal and very large, with four pairs of long, filamentous barbels. Eyes small, at the sides, towards front of head. Dorsal and anal fins very long, extending to tail, and composed entirely of soft rays. No adipose fin. Pectoral fins with a sharp, serrated spine that can be locked in position. Pelvic fins in midbody, tail fin rounded. Last pair of gill arches modified into tree-like air-breathing organs housed in bony cavities. Jaws with broad bands of fine, pointed teeth, with an additional vomerine tooth band behind the upper jaws on the palate. Coloration above and on the sides is dark grey-green to black, often mottled with irregular dark blotches; belly white. Belly and ends of fins flushed with red while spawning. Can reach 59 kg, but usually not more than 20 kg.

The second-largest freshwater fish in southern Africa after the vundu, *Heterobranchus longifilis*. One of the most adaptable and hardy African fishes, it is a dominant ecological presence wherever it occurs. A widespread air-breathing catfish that is common in almost all habitats, including mainstream channels and tributaries, lagoons, oxbow lakes, backwaters, floodplains and drying-up pools. A nocturnal and crepuscular omnivore and stalking predator that detects food using its long, sensory barbels and electroreception. Juveniles feed on fruits, snails, shrimps, crabs and small fish. Adults feed mainly on fish, but also eat fruits, berries, frogs, reptiles (including snakes and small crocodiles), birds or small mammals, and scavenge on carcasses and hippopotamus dung. Their wide mouths enable them to swallow relatively large prey whole.

Although they are generally slow swimmers, they can swim quickly and jump low rapids if necessary. Coordinated pack-hunting behaviour has been observed in the Okavango Delta during the annual 'catfish run', which occurs between September and November in the riverine panhandle. Thousands of catfish prey on shoals of small fish, mainly snoutfishes, which are forced off the floodplains by receding water levels. Catfish may also herd small cichlids into shallow water before catching them. In habitats with few large prey they are able to strain plankton from the water. Crocodiles are a major predator of catfish during the catfish run, as well as during the spawning migrations into shallow water, when traditional fishermen also catch large numbers of fish using spears and clubs. Their terrestrial predators include fish eagles, storks and leopards.

Spawning begins with the onset of rising floodwaters, when they migrate onto the floodplains or into the shallows of backwater lagoons. Males fight one another for the right to mate with ripe females. Courtship and egg laying take place at night, usually at new moon or after rain. The eggs, about 2 mm in diameter, stick to recently flooded plants in very shallow water (less than 20 cm). Hatching occurs within 24–36 hours. The larvae initially feed off their small yolk sacs but become free-swimming hunters within 3–4 days. Growth is rapid, with fishes reaching 200 mm SL within a year. Growth rates in females decline after about three years and most large fish are males. Sexual maturity may be reached after one year but usually takes two or more years. They live for eight years or more.

Sharptooth catfish are very tolerant of extreme environmental conditions and are often the last species to survive as lakes dry up. When Lake Ngami dried up in 1982/3, catfish were preyed on by marabou storks, baboons, hyaenas and other predators, as well as by fishermen, and tens of thousands of sharptooth and blunttooth catfish skulls littered the dry lake basin. In dry conditions they use their air-breathing organs once their gills collapse and are also able to crawl overland using their locked pectoral spines. Although they can survive in wet mud under a dry mud layer, they cannot aestivate in completely dry mud like lungfish do. Because they rely mainly on their air-breathing organs for oxygen, and need to rise to the water surface regularly to take a gulp of air, they drown if they are confined underwater by nets or traps. Despite their hardiness, they are vulnerable to insecticide sprays because of their air-breathing habit.

Found throughout the Okavango Delta and Chobe River. Elsewhere they occur in rivers, lakes and swamps throughout Africa and into the Middle East and Turkey; they have been introduced into South America. Sharptooth catfish are the most naturally widespread species of African freshwater fish, being found from the Umtamvuna River in the south to the Nile River in the north, and are probably the freshwater fish with the widest latitudinal range in the world. They have also extended their range through their ability to breathe air and waddle across land and, with the aid of anglers and fish farmers, now, as an invasive species, constitute a severe threat to indigenous fishes. Strict controls over their movement must therefore be enforced.

Sharptooth catfish are an important source of protein in Africa and are frequently caught in commercial and subsistence fisheries. They are smoked, salted, curried or dried by traditional fishermen. An innovative way of cooking them is to cake the gutted fish in wet mud and bake it over hot coals. Although they are often sluggish, sharptooth catfish can provide good sport for anglers. They are caught using flies, spoons, spinners or large hooks baited with grasshoppers, frogs, animal entrails, blue soap, bread or fish, especially small cichlids. It is best to use heavy tackle, as they often entangle the line in plants or logs. Once caught they also have a habit of making their way back into the water undetected!

This species was first collected in the Orange River by William Burchell in 1811 and was one of the first freshwater fish species to be described from southern Africa. In Burchell's day the Orange River was known as the 'Gariep' by the local people, hence the specific name *gariepensis*. This fish has over 100 common names throughout its range in Africa.

Blunttooth catfish   *Clarias ngamensis* Castelnau, 1861
Dituni (S), *Duni* (S), *Ndombi* (S)

Avg L: 500 mm, TL: 730mm; D 56–62; A 50–58. Body heavy, ellipsoid, elongate; head depressed, slightly narrower than that of the sharptooth catfish, and covered largely by bony plates forming a protective helmet. Broad terminal mouth with a single oval pad of blunt, granular teeth on the palate (vomer) of the upper jaw. (In the sharptooth catfish this tooth pad is usually split into two parts.) Four pairs of filamentous barbels. Long, soft-rayed dorsal and anal fins extend nearly to the tail-fin base. Soft-rayed dorsal fin followed by short, low adipose fin (absent in the sharptooth catfish). Pectoral spine robust, slightly curved and serrated. Possesses a large, accessory air-breathing organ composed of modified gill arches in a bony chamber above the gills. Colour highly variable, dark brown or grey, often marbled, cream or off-white below. Reaches 4 kg.

A bottom-dwelling, nocturnal, stalking predator that inhabits well-vegetated habitats in slow-flowing river channels, floodplains, backwater lagoons with soft substrates, and drying pools. It is common in both the perennially flooded and seasonal areas of the Okavango Delta and Chobe River. Eats mainly snails and freshwater mussels (bivalves), which are crushed using its blunt teeth and powerful jaws, as well as crabs, shrimps, insects and fish. Observed pack-hunting with the sharptooth catfish during the annual 'catfish runs' in the riverine panhandle.

Breeds in summer in the same way as (and sometimes together with) the sharptooth catfish after rain, or after the arrival of the annual flood, in the riverine panhandle and perennial swamp. In the southern delta breeding occurs between September and January, depending on the magnitude of the annual flood and the time that it takes to reach the seasonal waterways. Males grow faster than females and reach sexual maturity at about 250 mm TL. This species lives for 5–6 years. Like the sharptooth catfish, it is a very hardy air-breather that is one of the last species to survive in lakes or pools that are drying up.

Elsewhere occurs in the Kavango, Cunene, Kafue, upper Zambezi, Zambian Congo, Cuanza, Shire and lower Zambezi systems, and in east coast rivers as far south as the Phongolo in KwaZulu-Natal. Named after Lake Ngami, near which the first specimens were collected, and described in 1861 by the French consul Comte de Castelnau. Like the sharptooth catfish, this species is an important source of protein and features strongly in the commercial, recreational and subsistence fisheries. Caught by anglers using live fish bait and spoons.

Blotched catfish   *Clarias stappersii* Boulenger, 1915
Dituni (S), *Duni* (S)

Avg L: 150 mm, SL 410 mm; D 62–80; A 56–63. Body elongate, head large, oblong, bony and flattened. Long-based, soft-rayed dorsal and anal fins. Terminal mouth with four pairs of short barbels, pectoral fins with strong spines serrated along the outer edge. Accessory breathing organ in chamber above the gills is well-developed, with plate-like branches. Dorsal and anal fins extend to the tail, no adipose fin. Body heavily blotched in dark brown and black, lateral line a thick white stripe, head and belly light brown or off-white.

Found in fast-flowing, rocky habitats such as Popa Rapids on the Kavango River in Namibia, as well as in dense bogs and marshes. Only two specimens have been collected in the Kavango River above Shakawe during a multi-year fisheries survey in the 1980s and 90s. A nocturnal omnivore that feeds on small fish, aquatic invertebrates and their larvae and plant material. As with other air-breathing catfishes, the onset of the rainy season and rising floodwaters prompt their migration onto floodplains or into backwater lagoons, where they spawn. Courtship and egg laying take place at night, and the eggs adhere to submerged plants. Rare in the Okavango Delta and Chobe River, and collected only upstream of Shakawe; absent from the seasonal southern delta. Elsewhere found in the Zambian Congo, Kasai Congo, upper Zambezi, Kafue and Cunene systems. The southern limit of its distribution is the upper Okavango Delta.

Smoothhead catfish   *Clarias liocephalus* Boulenger, 1898
Dituni (S), *Duni* (S)

Avg L: 120 mm, SL: 282 mm; D 67–79; A 53–67. Body elongate with a short oval to rectangular head, snout broadly rounded, eyes wide on sides of head. Terminal mouth with four pairs of long barbels. Tooth plates relatively broad. Cheeks behind eyes bulge in adults. Air-breathing organ reduced to a simple branched structure. Pectoral spines short, serrated on outer edge, weak along inner edge. Coloration plain or mottled dark brown to black on the back and flanks, light brown below. Dark submarginal band and edge to dorsal, anal and tail fins.

Little is known about this small catfish that prefers flowing-water channels and rocky rapids in the Kavango River in Namibia, where it hunts on the bottom among stones and rocks. Absent from floodplains and non-rocky habitats in the lower reaches of the system, but it does inhabit papyrus- and reed-fringed habitats along river channels. Young fish feed on detritus, plants, adult and larval insects and small fish, while adults eat only fish. Spawning is similar to that of other air-breathing catfishes, with a peak during the summer rainy season, after the inundation of the floodplains that serve as nurseries. A northern headwater species that has not yet been found in the Okavango Delta or Chobe River but is included here, as it may occur there. Elsewhere it is found in the Zambian Congo, Cunene, upper Zambezi and Kafue systems and Lake Victoria. The southern limit of its distribution is the Kavango River in Namibia.

Snake catfish   *Clarias theodorae* Weber, 1897
Dituni (S), *Duni* (S)

Avg L: 120 mm, SL: 350 mm; D 71–94; A 60–89. Body slender and elongate, snake-like in appearance. Head very short with a small, terminal mouth and long barbels reaching behind the head. Long dorsal and anal fins reach to the tail, no adipose fin. Pectoral fin spine is serrated along outer and inner edges. Coloration dark brown to black, usually mottled, but may be plain. Lateral line a thin white stripe. Air-breathing organ reduced, with stubby branches.

This common, relatively small air-breathing catfish inhabits dense aquatic vegetation and papyrus and reed rootballs in slow-flowing river channels and floodplain lagoons; occasionally found in rocky rapids. Does not occur in open-water habitats. Feeds on aquatic and terrestrial insects, shrimps, small fish and plant material. Reaches sexual maturity at about 100 mm SL. Spawning is similar to that of other air-breathing catfishes, with peaks during the summer rainy season and after the arrival of the floodwaters, when the floodplains, which serve as nurseries, are inundated. Although their air-breathing organs are reduced, snake catfish are functional air breathers and can migrate across wet ground.

Distributed throughout the Okavango Delta and Chobe River. Elsewhere they occur in the upper Congo, Lake Malawi and Lake Tanganyika catchments, the Rufiji River and from the Cunene, upper and lower Zambezi, Kafue and Limpopo systems southwards to the Umfolozi River in KwaZulu-Natal. Caught in the subsistence fisheries in elongated constriction traps that are specially designed to catch this species and in small valve traps set in reed weirs. They are also caught by traditional fishermen using swamp worms (*Alma* species) threaded onto stiff grass stems and tied to a line (without a hook) dropped into shallow water. Interesting aquarium species. Described and named by Dr Max Weber in honour of his wife's niece, the Dutch artist Theodora Jacoba Sleeswijk. One of the first African fish to be named after a woman.

Broadhead catfish *Clariallabes platyprosopos* Jubb, 1964
Dituni (S), *Duni* (S)

Avg L: 250 mm, SL: 283 mm; D 73–82; A 56–63. Body elongate, with a large, very broad, depressed head (as wide as it is long) and bulging cheeks. Teeth on upper jaw and palate in two broad pads. Barbels long, reaching beyond the head. Pectoral spine barbed along outer and inner edges. Coloration mottled black or dark brown. Air-breathing organ vestigial or absent. Reaches 0.128 kg.

A bottom-dwelling, air-breathing catfish found in rocky rapids in the Kavango River above Popa Rapids, Namibia, and in the Cubango River, Angola. Juveniles feed on invertebrates, while adults feed on fish. Spawning is probably similar to that of other air-breathing catfishes, with a peak during the summer rainy season, when the floodplains are inundated. Little else is known about this species. Not, as yet, recorded from the Okavango Delta or Chobe River but included here as it may occur there. Elsewhere it is found in the upper Zambezi River at Sioma and at Katombora Rapids above Victoria Falls. Occasionally caught by anglers. The southern limit of its distribution is the Kavango River. Described as a new species by Rex Jubb, from specimens caught above Victoria Falls in the upper Zambezi River.

CLAROTEID CATFISHES Claroteidae

Relatively small catfishes with a large mouth, three or four pairs of barbels, one spine in the dorsal and pectoral fins and a well-developed adipose fin. Pelvic fins far back, tail fin rounded. Closely related to other African catfishes, particularly the schilbeids and mochokids. One species known from the region.

Zambezi grunter   *Parauchenoglanis ngamensis* (Boulenger, 1911)
Onxaa (B), *Thijatarmvu* (H)

SL: 380 mm; D I, 7; A iv–v, 8–9. Body cylindrical, head large and slightly flattened, with tapered snout and fleshy lips, eyes small, on top of head. Three pairs of unbranched, broad-based barbels, of which the outer barbel is the longest. Nostrils widely separated and positioned on the upper lip. Fine teeth on a kidney-shaped pad in the upper jaw and along the lower jaw. Strikingly marked: yellow-brown above, with scattered black spots arranged in a series of 5–7 vertical bars, silvery below, with black blotches; all fins spotted. Dorsal and pectoral fins with a spine, strongly serrated in the pectoral fins, adipose fin very large, extending to the caudal peduncle, tail fin rounded. Juveniles with bold vertical bars.

A predatory catfish that is uncommon in the delta but found in slow and moderately fast-flowing river channels as well as in perennially flooded, well-vegetated backwater lagoons, often sheltering under trees. Also found in slow-flowing habitats along the lower Boteti River. Like the squeakers, it grunts when removed from the water. Feeds on detritus, snails, insect larvae, shrimps and small fishes. Spawning takes place in September and October, after rain and during the annual flood, probably on shallow floodplains. Produces relatively few (less than 1,000), large eggs, which may be protected by the parents. Patchily distributed in the Okavango Delta and the Kavango and Chobe rivers. More common in the northern perennial swamp and uncommon in the southern seasonal swamp. Protected in the Moremi Game Reserve and Chobe National Park.

Elsewhere it is found in the upper Zambezi and Kasai Congo systems. The first specimens were collected by R. B. Woosnam near Lake Ngami, hence the specific name *ngamensis*. Its southern limit of distribution is the Okavango Delta. A potential aquarium species. Occasionally caught by anglers using earthworm bait and by subsistence fishermen in traps set in reed weirs. Vulnerable to gill netting because of its pectoral spines.

SQUEAKERS AND SUCKERMOUTHS   Mochokidae

Very diverse group of relatively small African catfishes. Named 'squeakers' for the distinctive sounds individuals make when removed from the water. Mouth oval or round and located underneath the head. Very strong pungent spines in the dorsal and pectoral fins. High dorsal fin, pectoral fins low on body, pelvic fins far back, tail fin forked in Botswana species. Large adipose fin present. Eight species known from the area.

Okavango suckermouth   *Chiloglanis fasciatus* Pellegrin, 1936

Avg L: 40 mm, SL: 50 mm; D I, 6; A iii–iv, 7. Body slender and tapered, tail fin forked. Head strongly downcurved and depressed, covered with thick skin, eyes relatively large. The pronounced ventral mouth forms a disc that is used to hold onto rocks and plants in river currents. Barbels moderately long. First dorsal fin with spine, second dorsal fin in the form of a smallish adipose fin located above the anal fin. Serrated pectoral fin spines. Off-white or light brown background colour with dark brown or black blotches on body, black bands across the tail fin.

A small catlet found in fast-flowing rocky reaches of large rivers and among fringing papyrus and reed mats. Common in the Popa Rapids on the Kavango River, Namibia. Observed 'hitchhiking' under floating papyrus mats that break away from mainstream channels during high floods and float downstream. Feeds on small invertebrates and algae from the surface of rocks and plants. Spawning occurs during the summer, coinciding with summer rains and the annual flood. Only known from the vicinities of Nxamaseri and Seronga in the perennial upper delta, unknown from the seasonal southern delta. Found in the riverine panhandle and Kavango River in Namibia and in the Kwando-Linyati-Chobe river system. Elsewhere occurs in the upper Zambezi River and its tributaries. The southern limit of its distribution is the northern Okavango Delta.

Spotted squeaker   *Synodontis nigromaculatus* Boulenger, 1905
Umkoko (S), *Nkokoko* (B), *Diwekeweke* (H)

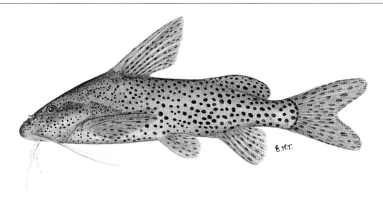

Avg L: 200 mm, SL: 300 mm; D I, 7; A iv–vi, 7–9. Body deep. Head bony with a triangular humeral process located behind the gill opening and pointing backwards. Mouth ventral, snout short, barbels long and slender, with lower-jaw barbels having filamentous branches. Dorsal fin tall, dorsal and pectoral fins with a hardened, serrated spine, tail fin forked. When alarmed, it erects and locks the spiny dorsal and pectoral fins to form a triangle that makes it difficult for predators to swallow. Coloration slate grey or olive-green, with entire body and all fins covered in small black spots. Like other squeakers, when disturbed it produces sounds by rubbing the base of the pectoral spine against the pectoral girdle.

A common and widespread flowing-water species of upside-down catfish, so called because it swims upside down beneath objects, such as logs, and at the water surface. Inhabits rocky habitats and papyrus and reed fringes along river channels and around perennial lagoons. Uncommon on seasonal floodplains. Feeds on detritus, algae, plant material, insects, snails and small fish. Spawning takes place during summer, with the peak coinciding with the rains and the arrival of the annual flood. The green eggs are deposited on plants. Distributed throughout the Okavango Delta, but more common in the perennial swamp and riverine panhandle. Also occurs in the Chobe River. Elsewhere it is known from the Congo, upper Zambezi and Kasai systems and Lake Tanganyika. The southern limit of its distribution is the Okavango Delta. Caught by subsistence fishermen. Usually regarded as a pest by anglers, who struggle to unhook squeakers without being pricked by their spines. Like other squeakers, it is vulnerable to gill nets due to its long, serrated dorsal and pectoral spines.

Upper Zambezi squeaker *Synodontis woosnami* Boulenger, 1911
Umkoko (S), *Nkokoko* (B), *Dimboto* (H)

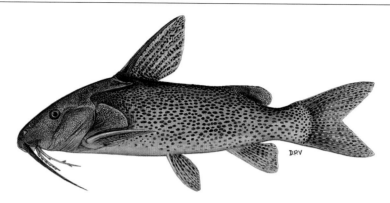

Avg L: 175 mm, SL: 205 mm; D I, 7; A v–vi; 7–9. Body elongate and triangular. Head large, snout prominent, mouth inferior. Main barbels short, with black inner membrane. Barbels from lower jaw with slender branches, humeral process broad and deep. Dorsal and pectoral fins with a strong serrated spine, tail fin forked. Colour creamish-white, typically with fine black spots on the upper body and flanks, underside of head and abdomen plain, head brown with fine speckling.

A squeaker that inhabits perennial river channels and open-water lagoons. Like all squeakers, it produces loud sounds when disturbed. Feeds on detritus, plant material, insects and snails. Spawning takes place during the summer, with a peak coinciding with the annual rains and the arrival of the flood. Patchily distributed in the Okavango Delta and Chobe River. Elsewhere it is found in the Cunene and upper Zambezi rivers. The southern limit of its distribution is the Okavango Delta.

Largespot squeaker *Synodontis macrostigma* Boulenger, 1911
Umkoko (S), *Nkokoko* (B)

Avg L: 150 mm, SL: 170 mm; D I, 7; A iv–vi, 7–9. Body stocky and triangular, with short snout. Mouth inferior. Upper jaw barbels with dark basal membrane and a papillose leading edge. Lower jaw barbels with short, stubby branches. Humeral process pointed. First dorsal fin with strong spine, second dorsal fin in the form of a large, rounded adipose fin. Pectoral fins with strong serrated spine, tail fin with shallow fork. Colour yellowish with characteristic large dark brown or black spots or dashes. Belly with smaller spots or plain. Head with small spots. All fins speckled or spotted.

A relatively common squeaker that prefers slow-flowing channels and floodplain environments. Inhabits river channels and open-water lagoons, especially with sandy substrates; occasionally found along rocky stretches or in deep water. Produces loud sounds when disturbed. Feeds on detritus, plant material, insects and snails. Spawning takes place during the summer, with a peak coinciding with the summer rains and the arrival of the annual flood. Long-lived: one of the authors (P.H.S.) has kept an individual in an aquarium for 25 years. Distributed throughout the Okavango Delta and in the Chobe River. Elsewhere it is found in the Cunene, Kavango, upper Zambezi and Kafue rivers. The southern limit of its distribution is the Okavango Delta. The common and specific names refer to its large body spots.

Largemouth squeaker   *Synodontis macrostoma* Skelton & White, 1990
Umkoko **(S)**, *Nkokoko* **(B)**, *Mphuto* **(B)**, *Dimboto* **(H)**

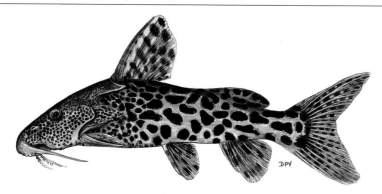

Avg L: 80 mm, SL: 92 mm; D I, 6; A v–vi, 7–8. Body triangular, snout long, with a large ventral mouth and a distinctive tooth pad on the upper jaw. Humeral process narrow, triangular and pointed. Upper jaw barbels simple, without basal membranes. Lower jaw barbels with short, stubby branches. First dorsal fin with strong spine, adipose fin rounded, moderately sized. Pectoral fins with serrated spine, tail fin forked. Background colour light creamish-brown, with small spots on the head. Body with variably sized spots and cloud-like black markings, underside plain or spotted. All fins spotted.

An uncommon nocturnal squeaker that inhabits rocky environments and the fast-flowing reaches of rivers, as well as flowing river channels lined with papyrus and reed beds. Produces loud sounds when disturbed. Feeds on small invertebrates and grazes on algae on rocks and plants. Spawning takes place during the summer, with a peak coinciding with the summer rains and rising floodwater levels. Distributed in the perennial riverine panhandle, the Kavango River in Namibia and the Chobe River. Elsewhere found in the Cunene, Kafue and upper Zambezi rivers. The southern limit of its distribution is the Okavango Delta. The specific name means 'big mouth'.

Leopard squeaker *Synodontis leopardinus* Pellegrin, 1914
Umkoko (S), *Nkokoko* (B)

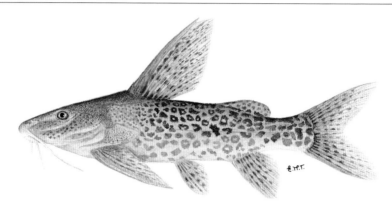

Avg L: 160 mm, SL: 196 mm; D I, 7; A v, 8–10. Body relatively slender, head profile straight to dorsal fin, body low and straight to the caudal fin. Snout short, mouth inferior. Barbels short, upper jaw barbels smooth or finely papillose, not reaching base of pectoral fin, basal membrane narrow, dark. Lower jaw barbel branches short and thick. First dorsal fin tall, the spine equal to head length, tail fin deeply forked. Pectoral fins with a strong serrated spine. Background colour light brown. Markings variable: usually small spots or slender stripes over the entire head and body, larger spots sometimes hollow. Belly plain or lightly spotted. Humeral process broad, triangular and pointed. Reaches 0.32 kg.

A common squeaker that inhabits large, open-water lagoons and slow-flowing rivers with backwaters and floodplains. Produces loud sounds when disturbed. Feeds on detritus, plant material, insects and snails. Spawning takes place during summer, with a peak coinciding with the summer rains and the arrival of the annual flood. Distributed throughout the Okavango Delta and Chobe River but more common in perennial habitats. Elsewhere known from the Kavango, upper Zambezi and Cunene rivers. The southern limit of its distribution is the Okavango Delta. Named for its leopard-like, spotted appearance.

Bubblebarb squeaker
Synodontis thamalakanensis Fowler, 1935

Umkoko (S), *Nkokoko* (B)

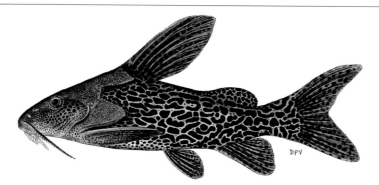

Avg L: 160 mm, SL: 175 mm; D I, 7; A v–vi, 8–9. Body triangular from above, cylindrical from the side. Dorsal fin very tall, longer than head length, tail fin forked. Humeral process large and rounded. Mouth ventral. Upper jaw barbels strongly papillose, with a broad black basal membrane. Lower jaw barbels with short, stubby branches. Background colour off-white, with an intricate pattern of variably shaped dark brown and black spots, squiggles and dashes.

An omnivorous squeaker that feeds on detritus, seeds, plant material, algae, insects, crustaceans and snails. Spawning takes place during summer, coinciding with the summer rains and the arrival of the annual flood, although it has been observed as early as July in the Namibian stretch of the Kavango River. Distributed throughout the Okavango Delta and Chobe River. Elsewhere it is found only in the Kavango and upper Zambezi systems. The southern limit of its distribution is the Okavango Delta. Named after the Thamalakane River where it was first collected. Common name refers to the bubble-like papillae on the upper jaw barbels.

Finetooth squeaker   *Synodontis vanderwaali* Skelton & White, 1990
Umkoko (S), *Nkokoko* (B)

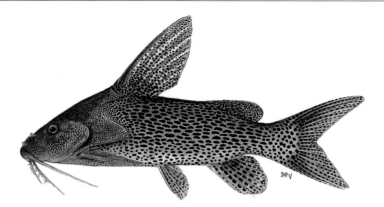

Avg L: 140 mm, SL: 160 mm; D I, 7; A v–vi, 7–9. Body triangular, snout short, tail fin forked. Large numbers of small teeth on the lower jaw and in the tooth pads on the upper jaw. Dorsal fin spine tall, about equal to head length. Upper-jaw barbels simple and long, extending beyond pectoral fin bases, with narrow, dark basal membranes. Lower-jaw barbels with short, stubby branches. Humeral processes broad, with a blunt tip, upper margin rounded. Background colour olive-brown, lighter below, and covered with numerous small dark brown or black dots and dashes that may merge to form stripes or a reticulated pattern. Head and fins lightly speckled.

A squeaker that prefers mainstream riverine environments. It produces loud sounds when disturbed. Feeds on detritus, plant material, insects and snails. Spawning takes place in summer, peaking with the summer rains and the arrival of the annual floods that inundate the floodplains and river fringes. Distributed in the Kavango River in Namibia and the Cubango River in Angola, but uncommon in the Chobe River. Elsewhere it is found in the Cunene and upper Zambezi systems. Named after Ben van der Waal, a fishery biologist who worked in the Caprivi Strip (now Zambezi Region) of Namibia for many years and made many collections of fishes for science. The species' common name refers to its many small teeth.

Distinctive catfishes, with a triangular body that is tapered and compressed from side to side. Mouth large. Dorsal and pectoral fins with sharp spines. Pectoral fins high on body, pelvic fins small. Tiny lobate adipose fin usually present. Anal fin very long, with more than 40 rays. Tail fin forked. Shoaling fishes, they swim in midwater, unlike other catfishes, which live on or near the bottom. One species known from the region.

Silver catfish   *Schilbe intermedius* Rüppell, 1832
Nkokoko (B), *Nxhoko* (B), *Leregi* (S), *Thideni* (H)

P. Skelton (NGOWP)

SL: 300 mm; D II, 5–6; A iv–v, 47–62. Body elongate, strongly compressed and tapered towards the tail. Head small, depressed, eyes large, on sides of head. Mouth large, terminal, with four pairs of thin filamentous barbels. Dorsal and pectoral fins far forward, each with a sharp serrated spine. Anal fin very long. No adipose fin present in Okavango or upper Zambezi populations. (A very small adipose fin is present in east coast river populations.) Tail fin sharply forked and droops downwards. Colour silvery or golden, with a large black blotch in the midline behind the head and dark brown, grey or black botches on the body. Juveniles frequently with three broad dark bands along body. Colour variable depending on water quality: lighter in turbid waters and darker, often mottled, in clear waters. Reaches 1.3 kg, females growing larger than males.

An abundant and widespread midwater species that usually shoals in slow-flowing river channels and open-water lagoons with emergent and submerged vegetation. More active at night or at dusk and dawn. Feeds on fish, frogs, crabs, snails, shrimps and winged termites that fall on the water surface, as well as on seeds and fruits, especially figs. Also feeds on hippopotamus dung and on rotting carcasses. Matures sexually at 160 mm SL and lives for 6–7 years. Spawns from September to November, after rain, in drainage rivers such as the Thamalakane and Boteti, and in backwater lagoons. Also spawns from February to March, during the annual flood, in the upper perennial swamp and riverine panhandle. Females lay their eggs on plants and do not guard them.

   Distributed throughout the Okavango Delta and Chobe River. Elsewhere silver catfish are found throughout tropical Africa, including the Nile and Senegal rivers in north and west Africa, and in the Cunene and Zambezi systems southwards to the Phongolo River in KwaZulu-Natal. Protected in the Moremi Game Reserve and Chobe National Park. An important species in commercial and subsistence fisheries in the Okavango Delta and Zambezi Region (Caprivi Strip). Frequently caught in small-mesh gill nets (24–60 mm stretched mesh). They are boiled, dried or smoked by traditional fishermen. Caught by anglers using flies, spinners and small spoons, or on small hooks baited with earthworms, grasshoppers, mealie meal pellets or pieces of fish or red meat. They produce very tasty fillets.

The silver catfish or butter barbel was previously regarded as two species, *Schilbe mystus* and *Eutropius depressirostris*. *Schilbe mystus* was one of the first African freshwater fish species to be described (1762) by the pioneering Swedish taxonomist Carolus Linnaeus, based on specimens collected in the Nile River. The specific name *mystus* means 'strange or weird' and *depressirostris* means 'depressed snout'.

SPINY EELS   Mastacembelidae

Long, slender, eel-like fishes from tropical Africa and Asia. Sharply pointed, fleshy snout, mouth under head. Skin smooth, with tiny scales. No lateral line. Dorsal, tail and anal fins joined, tail fin pointed. Pelvic fins absent, pectoral fins large, high on body. Related to the tropical swamp eels and not to true (anguillid) eels. Two species known from the region.

Longtail spiny eel   *Mastacembelus frenatus* Boulenger, 1901

SL: 400 mm; D XXVII–XXXIV, 69–81; A II, 66–83. Body very elongate and eel-like. Head and tail pointed. Mouth under head. Snout extended into a fleshy appendage with short tubular nostril openings. Dorsal fin very long, comprising a series of separate, short spines along the back followed by a long, soft dorsal fin that continues into the tail fin and anal fin under the body. Anal fin with two spines and extended soft-rayed section. Colour light or dark brown, with a dark brown reticulated pattern, and spots merging to form eye-spots on the tail.

A sedentary fish that inhabits dense papyrus and reed stands lining perennial river channels, as well as slow-flowing rapids among rocks and boulders. Also lives under floating papyrus mats within which it may be washed downstream. Found mainly in the riverine panhandle and perennial swamp, but an isolated population occurs among rocks at Matlapaneng Bridge on the Thamalakane River, in the lower seasonal swamp. Also found in the Chobe River. Ambushes its prey at night, by waiting for it to swim or drift within range before pouncing. Feeds on aquatic insects and their nymphs and on small fish. Breeds among aquatic plants in inundated areas during the flood season. Elsewhere it is found in the upper Zambezi and Kafue rivers, as well as in the Lufira–Congo River and the catchments of lakes Victoria and Tanganyika.

Ocellated spiny eel   *Mastacembelus vanderwaali* Skelton, 1976

SL: 180 mm; D XXII–XXVI, 64–75; A II, 64–79. Similar to the longtail spiny eel, but the dorsal fin has fewer spines, the head is larger, and the body coloration is bolder. Snout extended into a fleshy appendage, mouth under head. Head pointed, tail rounded. Body elongate and eel-like, but much deeper than that of the longtail spiny eel. Dorsal fin very long, with a series of short spines before the soft-rayed hind section. Two separate spines in front of the anal fin. Front nostril in the form of a fleshy snout appendage. Colour yellowish-brown, with a bold pattern of large dark brown or black blotches that merge to form a continuous scalloped band.

Originally found by Ben van der Waal, this uncommon fish was discovered living in crevices among rocky rapids, near Katima Mulilo in the Zambezi River. Feeds on insects taken from rocks. Occurs in the Kavango and upper Zambezi rivers. A potential aquarium species.

LABYRINTH FISHES Anabantidae

Tropical fishes from Africa and Asia. They can survive in swamps and streams with low oxygen concentrations owing to accessory air-breathing organs (labyrinths) housed in chambers above their gills. These labyrinths are a development of the first gill arch. These fishes have a long series of spines in the anal and dorsal fins. Pelvic fins well developed and far forward under the pectoral fins, which are high on the body. Tail fin is rounded, eyes large. Lateral line in two separate series, like cichlids. Unlike cichlids, they have two openings for the nostrils on each side of the snout and many (more than three) anal-fin spines. May breed by scattering their eggs. Alternatively, males may build a bubble nest on the water surface in which they guard the eggs and developing fry. Two species known from the region.

Blackspot climbing perch   *Microctenopoma intermedium* (Pellegrin, 1920)
Mbwindi (H)

SL: 62 mm; D XV–XVI, 8–9; A VIII–IX, 8–9. 25–30 ctenoid scales in lateral line, which is in two sections. Body slender, elongate. Head pointed, mouth small, terminal and upturned. Eyes large and far forward. Dorsal and anal fins long, tail fin rounded. Gill covers notched. Colour dark brown or black, with dark bars on the head radiating out from the eyes, and 7–13 dark bars on the body. Black spot on the caudal peduncle. Dorsal and anal fins black, with white lappets. Breeding males turquoise, with dark stripes.

An unusual fish that is able to extract oxygen from the air using an air-breathing organ in a chamber above the gills. This 'lung' consists of a thin, folded plate that is well supplied with blood vessels. The fish takes a gulp of air, which is forced into the lung chamber, where oxygen and carbon dioxide are exchanged. Inhabits the papyrus fringe along the main river channel as well as densely vegetated oxbow lakes and shallow floodplains in the perennial upper delta. Not recorded from the seasonal lower delta or from the southern drainage rivers. Well camouflaged and stealthy, it stalks its prey, feeding on the small aquatic nymphs of caddis flies and mayflies, as well as on periphyton, shrimps and fish fry.

Spawns in October and November after the first rains, and again in February and March during the annual flood. Males build a bubble nest on the water surface under which spawning takes place. The fertilized eggs float up into the nest and are guarded by the male. Distributed throughout the perennial reaches of the Okavango Delta and Chobe River. Elsewhere it is found in the Kavango, upper and lower Zambezi and Kafue systems and in the southern tributaries of the Congo River, as well as in iSimangaliso Wetland Park in KwaZulu-Natal. An interesting aquarium species.

Manyspined climbing perch   *Ctenopoma multispine* Peters, 1844
Mbondu (H), *Mbundu* (H), *Nvundo* (B), *Bontho* (B)

SL: 140 mm; D XVI–XIX, 8–9; A VIII–IX, 8–10. 30–32 ctenoid scales in lateral line, which is in two sections. Head covered with scales, hind edge of gill cover with strong spines, eyes large and far forward. Body elongate. Dorsal and anal fins long, tail fin rounded. The well-developed, tube-like air-breathing organs are located in a chamber above the gills. Upper body brown, with irregular dark brown or black zigzag bars and blotches. Belly lighter olive-brown, fins brown. Mature males have spines on the free edges of the cheek scales.

This well-camouflaged climbing perch inhabits densely vegetated riverine backwaters, swamps, lagoons (such as Maqwexana Pools and Dungu Lagoon), floodplains and isolated rain pools, where it preys on insect larvae, shrimps, snails and small fish. It is a hardy species that can survive in hot, stagnant water with little oxygen. After rain, it is able to shuffle on its side over wet ground, from one waterbody to another or in search of food, using the spines on its gill covers as levers. Local fishermen call it *bontho* ('the fish from the sky'), as they sometimes find it far from water after rain. Spawns between October and February following rain. Groups migrate to shallow water for spawning, sometimes moving overland at night to reach temporary pools. Their dark brown coloration provides effective camouflage in and out of water. The eggs are not guarded.

Widely distributed but uncommon in the Okavango Delta and Chobe River. Elsewhere they are found in the Kavango, Quanza, upper and lower Zambezi and Kafue systems, the southern tributaries of the Congo River and southwards in east coast rivers, lakes and swamps from Mozambique to the Kosi lakes, Lake Sibaya and the St Lucia wetland in northern KwaZulu-Natal. The specific name *multispine* refers to the spines on the gill cover. First collected by Dr Wilhelm Peters near Quelimane in Mozambique in the 1840s.

RIVER BREAMS, SARGOS, LARGEMOUTH BREAMS, HAPLOCHROMINES AND TILAPIINES

Cichlidae

A very diverse group of spiny-rayed fishes. Found in fresh and brackish water in Africa, the Middle East, South Asia, Madagascar and South America. Lateral line in two separate series. Scales present on head and body. Dorsal and anal spines well developed, three to four anal spines, pectoral fins large and high on body, pelvic fins far forward, below pectoral fins, tail fin rounded or truncate. Pelvic fins have a spine and five branched rays. All species perform some parental care of the eggs and fry and either lay and guard their eggs in nests or mouthbrood the eggs and young. Traditionally divided into two main groups in southern Africa: the plant- and detritus-eating tilapiines, and the predatory haplochromines. Young tilapiines have a dark spot at the base of the soft dorsal fin, and many adult haplochromines have a series of 'egg spots' on the anal fin. Many of the cichlids are protected within the Moremi Game Reserve and Chobe National Park. Most closely related to the marine damselfishes. Eighteen species known from the region.

Redbreast tilapia   *Coptodon rendalli* (Boulenger, 1897)

Ditapia (B), *Mampakibidu* (B), *Tlhapi* (B), *Nxhoro* (B), *Ngondu* (H), *Mmampakhibudu* (S)

TL: 400 mm; D XIV–XVI, 12–13; A III, 9–10. 28–32 scales in lateral line, which is in two sections. Body deep, head profile convex, mouth protruding, small, terminal. Adults olive-green to brown, with regular cross-meshed pattern, scattered blue scales, and 5–7 dark olive bars on the body. Juveniles with clear 'tilapia spot' on the dorsal fin. Throat and chest red, often extending to belly, dorsal fin with red margin. Distal edge of tail fin red or yellow. Juvenile coloration silver. Reaches 2 kg. Previously known as *Tilapia rendalli swierstae*.

Prefers quiet, well-vegetated lagoons and backwaters. Uncommon in fast-flowing water. A widespread and adaptable tilapia that is one of the few Okavango fishes to feed mainly on living plants. Adults often take characteristic semicircular bites out of floating water lily (*Nymphaea* spp.) leaves. They also eat algae, flying ants, crabs, shrimps and small fish. Juveniles feed on detritus and plankton. They reach maturity at 110–130 mm TL, and spawning takes place from September to December, among aquatic plants on the shallow fringes of lagoons and backwaters. The males dig large, shallow nests (50–1,500 mm across) in large colonies (leks). The nests often include deeper brood pits dug by the females in which the eggs are laid and the fry hide. Females lay between 3,000 and 8,000 small eggs at a time, 6–8 times a year. Both parents guard the nests. After reaching 15 mm TL the juveniles leave the pits and forage around the nest. They reach 210 mm TL by five years and 270 mm TL after eight years.

These tilapia are found in suitable habitats throughout the Okavango Delta and Chobe River. Elsewhere they occur in the Cunene, Kavango, Zambezi, Lualaba Congo and Zambian Congo systems, lakes Tanganyika and Malawi, and southwards through the east coast lakes, rivers and estuaries to the Phongolo River and Lake Sibaya in KwaZulu-Natal. This species is tolerant of a wide range of temperatures (11–37°C) and salinities of up to about 19 parts per thousand (more than half the salinity of sea water). Widely stocked in natural and manmade waters in South Africa and Zimbabwe, and important in aquaculture, as it readily takes artificial food. Also used for weed control in dams. Redbreast tilapia are important in the subsistence fishery and are a popular angling species. Although they are plant-eaters, they readily take earthworms, flying ants, algae, mealie meal or fish bait and can also be caught using small spinners or bass plugs.

Banded jewelfish *Hemichromis elongatus* (Guichenot, 1861)
Tlhapi (S), *Mondlhovu* (H), *Hagwa* (B)

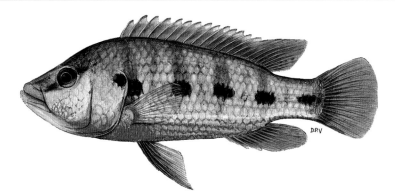

Avg L: 120 mm, SL: 190 mm; D XIII–XV, 11–13; A III, 8–10. 28–32 scales in lateral line, in two rows. Body elongate. Head large, profile slightly concave. Mouth terminal, large with two distinctive conical teeth in front of upper jaw. Dorsal fin long, reaching caudal peduncle. Pelvic fins far forward, under pectoral fins. Anal fin large. Tail fin large, truncate and rounded. Body dark olive above, with 4–5 black blotches extending into bars along the lateral midline, and faint olive-green vertical bars. Black-and-red spots on upper gill cover, oblique black bands across the eyes. Belly and underside of head red, brighter in breeding males. Dorsal, anal and tail fins dark olive, pelvic fins black, pectoral fins transparent. Mature males are larger and more colourful than females and also develop elongated dorsal and anal fins.

A common predatory cichlid that is often found alone. Inhabits the edges of slow-flowing river channels; also occurs in seasonal and perennial lagoons with clear water and aquatic vegetation. More common in the riverine panhandle and perennial upper swamp than in the seasonal lower swamp. Found in Dungu and Gomuto lagoons in the riverine panhandle and in Chanogha and Nxaragha lagoons in the seasonal delta. A nocturnal predator that preys on shrimps, insects and small fish. Males and females pair off to breed during summer, at the onset of the rainy season. Only about 500 large eggs are produced for each spawn. The adults make a sand-scrape nest where the eggs are fertilized, and both parents guard the eggs and fry. Occurs throughout the Okavango Delta and in the Kavango, Kwando and Chobe rivers. Elsewhere found in West African rivers and in the upper Congo and upper Zambezi systems. Its southern limit of distribution is the Okavango Delta. Caught in the subsistence fishery. Readily takes worm or fish bait. An attractive but aggressive aquarium species that readily breeds in captivity.

Threespot tilapia *Oreochromis andersonii* (Castelnau, 1861)
Ditapia (B), *Empaa* (B), *Thlapi* (S), *Mbweya* (H)

P. Skelton

TL: 500 mm; D XVI–XVIII, 11–14; A III, 11–13. 31–35 scales in lateral line, which is in two sections. Deep-bodied, with a rounded snout and small, terminal mouth. Juveniles silvery, with 8–9 bars and 3–4 spots in midbody. Adults are blue-grey, with light scale borders creating a mesh pattern. Fins blue-grey, with white spots on the soft dorsal and anal fins. Margins of dorsal, anal and tail fins bright red. Breeding males blue-black, with a silvery mesh, maroon on top of head, upper dorsal and tail fins bright red. Three body spots are usually visible from an early age. Reaches 3.2 kg. **Vulnerable**

A large and abundant tilapia that inhabits slow-flowing river channels and quiet lagoons and coves with dense aquatic plant cover. Adults live in deep, open waters, whereas juveniles and sub-adults prefer shallow floodplain lagoons, marshes and small tributaries. It is a detritivore that feeds on fine particulate matter, including algae, diatoms, detritus and zooplankton, with larger fish also eating insects and other invertebrates. Its natural predators include tigerfish, southern African pike, catfishes and fish-eating birds, including fish eagles, storks and herons.

The threespot tilapia is a hardy species that was one of the last cichlids to survive habitat desiccation when Lake Ngami dried up in 1982. It is also one of the first species to colonize newly flooded habitats. In habitats where the water has a low oxygen content shoals of threespot tilapia practise 'finning', by swimming along the water surface and gulping oxygenated water from the surface layer, with their fins out of the water. This occurs on hot, overcast days when respiration by aquatic plants (which use oxygen) exceeds the rate of photosynthesis (which produces oxygen). Finning also takes place when strong winds mix the anoxic bottom sediments, which contain hydrogen sulphide, with the rest of the water column, which also reduces oxygen levels in the water.

They normally start breeding at around 300 mm TL, when they are about four years old, although in the harsh conditions of the seasonal swamp, some fish grow rapidly and breed at 150 mm TL. Males excavate large, bowl-shaped nests in the sand, in water 1–3m deep, with up to 40 nests spaced closely together in breeding arenas or leks. The male attracts ripe females to the nest where the eggs are released and fertilized. The female gathers them up and mouthbroods the eggs and fry for about two weeks. The male continues to defend the nest and attract further females. Multiple broods are raised during the warmer months. Lives for 7–8 years.

Distributed throughout the Okavango Delta and Chobe River. Elsewhere threespot tilapia are found in the Cunene, Kavango, upper and middle Zambezi and Kafue systems. Their southern limit of distribution is the Okavango Delta. A very important fish in the subsistence and commercial fisheries and a valuable aquaculture species; a threespot tilapia farm has been established near Kasane in northeast Botswana. A popular angling fish that is caught using earthworm bait and on small spinners and spoons. A related species, the Nile tilapia (Oreochromis niloticus), has invaded the upper Zambezi River from fishponds in Zambia and has the potential to hybridize with and eliminate pure stocks of the threespot (and greenhead) tilapia in the Okavango Delta and Chobe River. Every effort should be made to prevent this from happening. Named after the Swede Charles John Anderson, who explored Namibia in the middle of the 19th century, enduring incredible hardships and eventually dying on the Cunene

River. First collected in the 1850s from Lake Ngami by Frederic Daviaud, an assistant to Comte de Castelnau, French consul in Cape Town, who described the species.

Greenhead tilapia   *Oreochromis macrochir* (Boulenger, 1912)
Ditapia (B), *Tlhapi* (S), *Ntarti* (H), *Ntshu* (B)

TL: 400 mm; D XV–XVII, 11–14; A III, 9–12. 31–32 scales in the lateral line, which is in two sections. Head profile rounded, mouth small and terminal. Body deep, pectoral fins long. Adults olive to iridescent green above, with silver-grey flanks and fins. Dark markings and spots on the head, gill covers and dorsal surface. Dorsal fin with a red-and-yellow margin and sooty green spots on the soft membranes. Breeding males bright green on the head and upper body, with prominent white genital tassels. Juveniles silvery, with 8–9 thin bars on the body and yellowish fins. Reaches 2.6 kg, with males growing larger than females. **Vulnerable**

An abundant tilapia that inhabits quiet waters along river margins and in floodplains and backwater lagoons, such as Maqwexana Pools, with dense aquatic plants. They feed on phytoplankton, especially the alga *Microcystis*, as well as plant material, insect nymphs and detritus, algae, desmids and diatoms collected from bottom sediments. Spawning takes place between September and March, in shallow water. The males dig and guard a nest with a central, volcano-shaped mound. The top, which is slightly concave, round or star-shaped, serves as the mating platform. Males court several females in succession, and the females mate with more than one male in a season. Several nests are often grouped into a breeding arena or lek. The females release about 400 eggs per spawning and mouthbrood the fertilized eggs and fry, while the males continue to guard the nests and attract additional females.

Distributed throughout the Okavango Delta and Chobe River. Elsewhere found in the Cunene, Kavango, upper Zambezi, Kafue and Congo systems, and widely stocked beyond their natural range in Zambia and Zimbabwe. Their southern limit of distribution is the

Okavango Delta. They are important to the subsistence and commercial fisheries and in aquaculture. Popular angling fish, they are caught using earthworms or filamentous alga bait. The specific name *macrochir* means 'large hand' and refers to the long pectoral fins. First collected by Tom Codrington in the upper Zambezi River, just above Victoria Falls.

Zambezi river bream   *Pharyngochromis acuticeps* (Steindachner, 1866)
Tlhapi (S), *Ditungungwa* (H), *Sikamakhodje rhe muklhumu* (B)

TL: 220 mm; DXIV–XVI, 10–13; A II, 7–10. 31–36 scales in the lateral line, which is in two sections. Head large, snout rounded, mouth slightly oblique. Body slender, with a straight profile. Dorsal fin long. Tail fin truncate. Body brown above with dark brown bars, iridescent green below. Scales with red centres. Dorsal and anal fins with red spots on soft-ray sections, tail fin with dark brown spots, anal fin with orange egg-spots. Chest of breeding males sooty grey.

A moderate-sized species that is abundant in the fringes of slow-flowing river channels and tributaries, lagoons, and sawgrass floodplains with abundant aquatic plants or tree roots. Feeds on snails, including freshwater mussels, shrimps and insect larvae, and on the eggs and fry of nesting fishes. Its predators include cormorants and darters. Spawns in early summer. A mouthbrooder, with the female carrying as many as 800 eggs and fry in her mouth. Lives for 3–4 years. Occurs throughout the Okavango Delta and in the Kavango and Chobe rivers. Elsewhere found in the Cunene, upper and middle Zambezi and Kafue systems and in the upper Save–Runde system in Zimbabwe. Caught in the subsistence fishery. A potential aquarium species.

Southern mouthbrooder *Pseudocrenilabrus philander* (Weber, 1897)
Molomo sekausu (B), *Tlhapi* (S), *Kapande* (H)

P. Skelton

TL: 130 mm; D XIII–XVI, 9–11; A III, 7–9. 27–30 scales in the lateral line, which is in two sections. Head and mouth large. Body stout, tallest at the back of the head and tapered towards the tail. Mouth terminal, large. Eyes large. Dorsal fin long. Pectoral fins short and rounded. Pelvic fins far forward, under the pectoral fins. Anal fin large. Tail fin rounded. Marked sexual dimorphism. Females light brown, with faint vertical bars and yellowish fins. Males iridescent light blue and yellow, with iridescent blue lower jaw. Oblique bar through the eye in both sexes. Pelvic fins black. Dorsal, anal and tail fins with blue or red blocks. Anal fin with orange tip. Males larger than females.

An extremely common small cichlid, with wide environmental tolerances. Inhabits slow-flowing rivers and tributaries, backwater lagoons and sawgrass floodplains. Prefers to remain close to the substrate in vegetated zones. The young feed on zooplankton, whereas the adults eat plant material, insects, zooplankton and small fish, including the juveniles of large species. Also takes insects on the water surface, such as ants or termites. Predators include kingfishers and cormorants. Breeds from early spring to late summer. Males aggressively defend a territory and use their mouths to make a simple, saucer-shaped nest to which they attract ripe females. The eggs are laid in the nest, fertilized by the male, and then collected and brooded in her mouth by the female in a secluded nursery area. The fry gradually spend more time out of the mother's mouth and become free swimming after about two weeks. Several broods are raised in a season. Lives for 4–5 years.

Distributed throughout the Okavango Delta and in the Kavango and Chobe rivers. Elsewhere found in Lake Malawi and the Congo River, southwards to the Orange and Uvongo rivers, and in the coastal lakes of KwaZulu-Natal. Frequently caught in the subsistence fishery. First collected from KwaZulu-Natal in the 1890s. The specific name *philander* refers to the fact that the male may take many partners (polygamy). An attractive but aggressive aquarium fish that readily breeds in captivity.

Rainbow bream
Sargochromis carlottae (Boulenger, 1905)
Tlhapi (S), *Ozizi* (B)

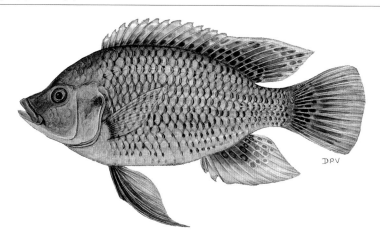

TL: 260 mm; D XIV–XVI, 11–13; A III, 9–11. 28–32 scales in the lateral line, which is in two sections. Head small, mouth terminal, eyes large. In adults body deep, with body depth greater than head length. Forehead rounded, with a concave head profile. Tail fin rounded. Juveniles silvery-green, with dark grey centres to the body scales and about eight dark vertical bars. Fins greyish-green, with grey spots. Adults olive-green, with dark-bordered scales forming a mesh pattern. Median fins deep olive, with brown spots. Pelvic fins sooty. Orange-pink egg-spots on the anal fin. Can reach 1.4kg, males growing larger than females.

An uncommon species that favours deeper floodplain channels and lagoons. Feeds on snails (including the snail hosts of bilharzia), crustaceans and aquatic insects. Matures sexually at 1–2 years and 100–120 mm SL. Lives for 5–6 years. Spawns multiple times during summer. The males dig a small sand-scrape nest in which 250–500 eggs are laid and fertilized. The females mouthbrood the eggs and fry. Distributed sparsely in the Okavango Delta and Chobe River. Elsewhere it is found in the Kafue and upper and middle Zambezi systems, including Lake Kariba. The southern limit of its distribution is the Okavango Delta. An important species in gill-net fisheries. Used as a snail-control agent in several southern African waterbodies. The first specimen was collected from the upper Zambezi River, near Victoria Falls, by W.L. Sclater, a former director of the South African Museum in Cape Town. George Boulenger named the species after Sclater's wife, Charlotte.

Dusky bream
Sargochromis codringtonii (Boulenger, 1908)
Tlhapi (S)

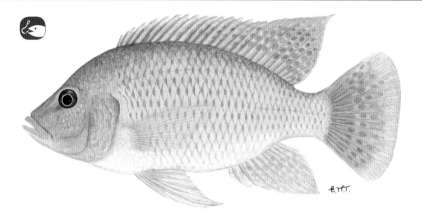

TL: 290mm; D XIV–XVI, 12–14; A III, 8–10. 34–35 scales in the lateral line, which is in two sections. Body deep with straight or slightly concave head profile. Eye width moderate, 4–5 x in head length. Mouth short, not reaching to below anterior orbit, terminal, slightly inclined. Dorsal fin deep; soft-rayed portion to pointed tip, tail fin truncate. Colour of juveniles and non-breeding adults olive-green, with deep red spots at the base of the scales and scale centres light, forming series of light parallel stripes. Pectorals light. Pelvics with dark leading edge. Median fins dark grey. Adult females dusky grey-black with light off-white belly. Breeding males dark olive-green to black with red margins to dorsal and caudal fins and large light red ocelli on the anal fin. Reaches 2.21 kg.

Juveniles and sub-adults often confused with the same of the green bream. An uncommon species that inhabits deep, slow-flowing river channels and floodplain lagoons. Feeds on water lily seeds, plants, insects, snails (gastropods and mussels) and small fish. Spawns at least twice in summer. The males scrape a nest in the sand, and the females mouthbrood the eggs and fry. Patchily distributed in the Okavango Delta and Chobe River. Elsewhere it is found in the Kavango, upper and middle Zambezi and Kafue systems. The southern limit of its distribution is the Okavango Delta. An important species in the subsistence fishery and a fine angling fish that is caught using spinners or on hooks using worms or snail flesh as bait. Useful for bilharzia and snail control. First collected in 1907 above Victoria Falls by Tom Codrington.

Pink bream *Sargochromis giardi* (Pellegrin, 1903)
Tlhapi (S), *Mpa* (B), *Mbaya* (H), *Nkusha* (H)

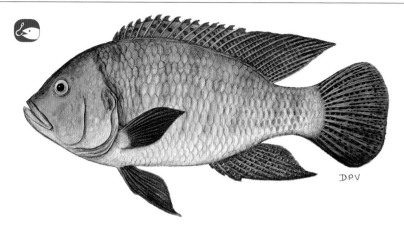

TL: 480 mm; D XIV–XVI, 12–15; A III, 9–11. 29–34 scales in the lateral line, which is in two sections. Body deep, heavyset. Head with a rounded forehead. Mouth terminal, inclined. Juveniles olive-green, with 6–7 vertical bars and a yellow chest. Adults greyish-green on back and head, with flanks and underparts creamy yellow. Fins dark green or dark grey, with red margins and dark red spots. Anal fin with rows of bright yellow, orange-centred egg-spots. Reaches 2.9 kg.

A floodplain specialist in the Okavango Delta and Chobe River system. Inhabits river channels and floodplain lagoons with sandy bottoms and lush vegetation. Feeds mainly on snails, bivalves and insect larvae, which it grinds up using its blunt throat teeth. Spawns in early summer. The male makes a nest, 200–300 mm in diameter, by clearing round patches of sand among underwater plants at a water depth of 1–2 m. The female mouthbroods the eggs and fry. This species reaches sexual maturity after 2–3 years, when it measures 150–180 mm TL, and lives for 6–7 years. Distributed throughout the Okavango Delta and Chobe River. Elsewhere found in the Kavango, Cunene, upper and middle Zambezi and Kafue systems. Its southern limit of distribution is the Okavango Delta. An important species in the subsistence fishery and regularly caught in gill nets by commercial fishermen. Also a popular angling fish and a useful snail-control agent. The first specimens were collected by the Czech explorer Emil Holub, in the Chobe River in the 1870s, and the species was named by the French zoologist Jacques Pellegrin.

Green bream   *Sargochromis greenwoodi* (Bell-Cross, 1975)

TL: 300 mm; D XIV–XVI, 12–14; A III, 8–10. 29–34 scales in the lateral line, which is in two sections. Body deep, obliquely ellipsoid, deepest at origin of dorsal fin. Head profile straight, mouth terminal, moderately large, oblique, reaching to below anterior orbit. Pelvic fins far forward, under the origins of the pectoral fins, tail fin truncate. Colour green to olive-green, with two black bands and about eight faint vertical bars. Dorsal and caudal fins dark grey-green with deep maroon blocks on membranes, lower tail fin reddish. Breeding males dark, with red edges to the dorsal fin, yellow margins to anal fin and yellow-orange egg-spots.

Often confused with juveniles and sub-adults of the dusky bream. Inhabits still or slow-flowing water with dense aquatic vegetation. Feeds primarily on snails, aquatic insects and small fish. Spawns in summer, and females mouthbrood the eggs and fry. Occurs in the Kavango River, Okavango Delta, Chobe River, upper and middle Zambezi and Kafue systems. A small component of the subsistence fishery. Named after the legendary British ichthyologist, Humphry Greenwood (1927–1995), who participated in several Okavango Delta research expeditions in the 1980s.

Humpback largemouth   *Serranochromis altus* Winemiller & Kelso-Winemiller, 1991
Tlhapi (S)

TL: 560 mm; D VI–XVI, 15–18; A III, 11–13. 37–39 scales in the lateral line, which is in two sections. Body very deep, with distinctly humped back and deeply concave forehead. Mouth large, sharply upturned, strongly protrusible. Olive-brown, with silver flanks. Scales with dark brown centres, giving a chequered look. Head plain olive-grey. Dorsal and tail fins with red spots and yellow or orange edges. Anal fin with large pink egg-spots. One of the biggest largemouth breams in southern Africa, reaching 3.9 kg.

A predatory cichlid found in fringing vegetation on the edges of main river channels and in deep lagoons connected to river channels. Fairly common but never abundant. Mainly active at night or at dusk and dawn, it feeds primarily on fish that are active at low light levels, such

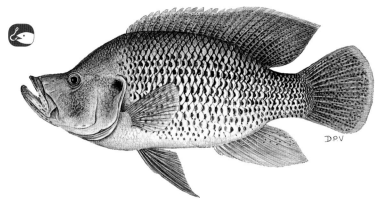

as snoutfishes and silver catfish. Reaches sexual maturity at about 300 mm TL and breeds in early summer before the rains, with the females mouthbrooding the eggs and fry. Distributed throughout the Okavango Delta and Chobe River but more common in perennially flooded habitats. Elsewhere found in the Kavango, Kafue and upper Zambezi systems. Its southern limit of distribution is the Okavango Delta. An important species in the floodplain fishery and a popular angling fish.

Thinface largemouth   *Serranochromis angusticeps* (Boulenger, 1907)
Tlhapi (B), *Mpwere* (B), *Molomosekausu* (S)

TL: 410 mm; D XIII–XVI, 14–17; A III, 11–13. 36–39 scales in the lateral line, which is in two sections. Head and body greatly compressed. Head concave in adults. Mouth very large, protrusible and sharply inclined. Teeth fine. Eyes small. Head and body with red and brown spots on a light brown to yellowish background. Breeding males have a bright yellow head; tail and dorsal fins blue-grey with dark brown spots; anal fin yellow-grey with orange egg-spots; black belly. Reaches 2.195 kg.

A common and widely distributed predatory cichlid in slow-flowing, deep, well-vegetated habitats but also found in the fast-flowing reaches of rivers and channels over sand and rocks. Occurs along the margins of mainstream river channels and in most of the larger, perennial lagoons, such as Xakanaxa, Gadikwe and Xobecqa. Also found in Nxaragha Lagoon on the Boro River and Chanogha Lagoon on the Boteti River. A diurnal ambush predator that feeds mainly on shrimps, aquatic and terrestrial insects, snails and small fish, especially robbers, topminnows, barbs and snoutfishes. Its thin shape allows it to stalk prey among the upright stems of water plants, where its red spots and general coloration provide effective camouflage.

Spawning takes place throughout the year in different parts of the Okavango Delta and Chobe River, except in the cooler winter months from May to July. The males dig shallow sand-scrape nests among plants, at depths of 1–3 m. The females mouthbrood the eggs and fry, after which the juveniles migrate into shallow nursery areas, on the floodplains or in backwaters, until the floodwaters recede and force them into perennial waterways. They reach sexual maturity after 1–2 years, at about 175 mm TL (females) and 250 mm TL (males), and live for 8–9 years.

Distributed throughout the Okavango Delta and Chobe River. Elsewhere they are found in the Cunene, Kavango, Zambian Congo, upper Zambezi and Kafue systems and are common in the Kafue Marsh and Bangweulu Swamp. A few specimens have been taken in the middle Zambezi, in Lake Kariba. Their southern limit of distribution is the Okavango Delta. An important species in the floodplain subsistence fishery and commercial gill-net fishery, and a very popular angling fish, as it is a good fighter. Can be caught close to the bottom in deep water using worms or live fish, bass plugs, spinners, or spoons with a steel trace. First collected from a coastal river near Moçamedes in Angola. The specific name *angusticeps* means 'narrow head'.

Longfin largemouth   *Serranochromis longimanus* (Boulenger, 1911)
Tlhapi (S)

TL: 300 mm; D XIV–XV, 13–14; A III, 9–10. 35 scales in the lateral line, which is in two sections. Deep-bodied, with a large, pointed head and large eyes. Mouth terminal, large and strongly upturned. Head profile straight or slightly concave. Very elongate pectoral fins extend past the origin of the anal fin (as do the pelvic fins). Other fins also long. Very distinctive, bold black-and-white colour pattern. Background coloration silvery-white; head and body with large black or dark brown blotches, combining into bars on the body. Four blotches radiate out from the eyes. Throat and belly yellow-white. Dorsal, anal and tail fins dark with light spots. Pectoral and pelvic fins dark brown or black. Anal fin of males with red egg-spots. Breeding males with iridescent green sheen on the body, gold-red colour dorsally and tail fin edged in red.

An uncommon predatory cichlid that inhabits perennial floodplain lagoons and backwaters in the perennial and seasonal delta.Occurs in Dungu and Gomuto lagoons in the riverine panhandle north of Seronga, as well as in Nxaragha (Boro River) and Chanogha (Boteti River) lagoons in the south. It is a nocturnal predator on aquatic insects, especially dragonfly nymphs, and also eats small fish.

Spawning occurs in summer, at the onset of the rainy season. The male makes a sand-scrape nest into which the female deposits a few large eggs (300–500), which are then fertilized. She mouthbroods the eggs and fry. The young reach sexual maturity at about 150 mm. They grow relatively slowly and reach about 260 mm in five years. Their distribution is limited to deeper lagoons in the perennial and seasonal delta and to deep channels in the Chobe River. Elsewhere they have been reported from floodplain lagoons in the upper Zambezi River. Their southern limit of distribution is the Okavango Delta. Rarely caught in the subsistence or sport fisheries. The first specimens were collected by R.B. Woosnam near Lake Ngami in 1910. The specific name *longimanus* means 'long-handed' and refers to the long pectoral fins.

Purpleface largemouth   *Serranochromis macrocephalus* (Boulenger, 1899)
Tlhapi (S)

SL: 350 mm; D XIV–XVI, 13–15; A III, 9–11. 34–37 scales in the lateral line, which is in two sections. Head large, with a straight profile. Mouth terminal, large and slightly upturned. Pectoral fins long but do not reach the origin of the anal fin. Colour highly variable: olive-brown with grey-black body bars; males with red edges to the dorsal, tail and anal fins. Breeding males are dark olive, with a purple flush on the head. Anal fin of male with large orange egg-spots that turn bright red during the spawning season. Reaches 2.13 kg.

A predatory cichlid that is common in habitats ranging from the papyrus- or reed-lined fringes of rivers and tributary channels, to floodplains, perennially flooded lagoons and backwaters with abundant aquatic vegetation. Preys on shrimps, snails, insects (especially midges) and small fish (especially snoutfishes, barbs and small cichlids, such as the banded tilapia). In the riverine panhandle, spawning takes place from October to November, at low water, before the annual floods arrive. Produces relatively few (200–250) but large eggs that are laid and fertilized in a sand-scrape nest made by the male. The female mouthbroods the eggs and fry, often under papyrus mats. Reaches sexual maturity within 1–2 years, at about 150 mm SL, and lives for 5–6 years.

Found mainly in the perennially flooded northern regions of the Okavango Delta, but also occurs in deeper, seasonally flooded waterways in the southern delta in Xo Flats, Nxaragha Lagoon (Boro River) and Chanogha Lagoon (Boteti River). It has also been found in isolated, turbid floodplain lagoons that are devoid of plants. Elsewhere occurs in the Kavango, Cunene, Congo, upper Zambezi and Kafue systems and in Lake Kariba on the middle Zambezi River. Its southern limit of distribution is the Okavango Delta. An important species in the subsistence fishery and a popular angling fish that is caught using worms as bait, or with a small lure. The specific name *macrocephalus* means 'large-headed'.

Nembwe *Serranochromis robustus* (Günther, 1864)
Tsungwa (S), *Mbonje* (H), *Nxlhaa* (B), *Robbie* (Zimbabwe)

SL: 450 mm; D XV–XVI, 13–15; A III, 10–11. 36–39 scales in the lateral line, which is in two sections. Body robust. Mouth terminal and large, teeth conical. Eyes large. Pectoral fins short. Colour olive to bright green, with a deep olive band along the body. Fins olive, with yellow to orange margins. Anal fin of males with small orange egg-spots. Breeding males have a deep yellow chest and belly, and a yellow-flushed anal fin. Typically reaches 3.5 kg, but a specimen of 6.123 kg has been reported from Zimbabwe.

A relatively large and common predatory cichlid. Inhabits perennial river channels, adjacent coves and backwater lagoons, over both sandy and rocky substrates. Found in still water as well as in moderate currents, especially around logs, overhanging plants or floating papyrus mats. Also hunts at the confluences between main river channels and their tributaries. Juveniles live in shallower water in floodplain channels and backwater lagoons and feed on insects and small fish, such as minnows. Adults eat fishes, especially squeakers, but also barbs, striped robbers, small cichlids and catfishes, as well as crabs, shrimps, insects and snails. They often form hunting shoals, which forage in mainstream channels following the catfish runs (October–December), gorging themselves on the small fish that were not eaten by the catfish.

Spawning takes place in summer. The male makes a large nest in the sand among the papyrus fringing river channels or lagoons. The eggs are deposited and fertilized in the nests, which may be up to 400 mm in diameter and 100 mm deep. The female mouthbroods the eggs and fry in the papyrus fringe. Reaches about 400 mm TL after five years.

Nembwe are common in the perennial northern swamp and Chobe River but are uncommon in the seasonal southern swamp. Elsewhere they occur in the Cunene, Kavango, Kafue, Zambian Congo and upper and middle Zambezi systems, although they have also been widely stocked in lakes and dams. The southern limit of their natural distribution is the Okavango Delta. They are very important in the subsistence gill-net fishery and probably the most exciting cichlid target for anglers, who catch them using bass plugs, artificial worms, wet or dry flies, live fish or earthworms. They are also caught on spinners or one-hooked silver-and-copper spoons that are worked near the bottom, or next to rocks or logs, or else are allowed to drift downstream of rocky rapids, from turbulent to calm water. First collected by a missionary, Reverend Jalla, from the upper Zambezi River near Kazungula.

Brownspot largemouth *Serranochromis thumbergi* (Castelnau, 1861)
Tlhapi (S), *Mbonje* (H), *Njeyi* (B)

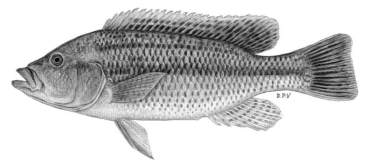

TL: 330 mm; D XVII–XVIII, 13–16; A III, 9–12. 39–41 scales in the lateral line, which is in two sections. Body slender and elongate. Dorsal fin spine count high. Lateral line scales clearly visible. Head and eyes large. Mouth large and terminal, slightly upturned. Pectoral fins short. Tail fin truncate or slightly concave. Head green. Body green-brown above, brown below, with off-white belly. Males with rust red centres on the body scales, creating a chequered pattern. Black band along the body except in breeding females. Males with orange egg-spots on the anal fin. Reaches 1.2 kg.

A predator that inhabits slower flowing river channels and lagoons with abundant aquatic plants. Like many other predatory cichlids, their habitat preferences are strongly influenced by the presence or absence of tigerfish. If tigerfish are absent, brownspot largemouths (and other largemouths) will hunt in open water, whereas, if tigerfish are present, they confine their hunting to the vegetated fringes of lagoons, smaller river channels and floodplains. They feed on insects, shrimps, crabs, snails and small fish (such as barbs, robbers and topminnows), which are caught near the water surface. Their predators include fish eagles and large catfish.

The male makes a sand-scrape nest, and the females brood the eggs and fry in their mouths. Patchily distributed in channels, lagoons and floodplains in the perennial upper swamp and in the Chobe River and its floodplain. Elsewhere occurs in the Cunene, Kavango, upper Zambezi, Kafue and Zambian Congo systems. Their southern limit of distribution is the Okavango Delta. An uncommon species in the subsistence fishery, but they are occasionally caught by anglers using worms, grasshoppers or live fish for bait or using small silver spoons. First collected near Lake Ngami by F. Daviaud in the 1850s. Although misspelt 'thumbergi', it was named for C.P. Thunberg, a Swedish botanist who travelled extensively in southern Africa in the 1770s.

Okavango tilapia   *Tilapia ruweti* (Poll & Thys van den Audenaerde, 1965)
Ditapia (B), *Tlhapi* (S), *Thingu* (H)

TL: 120 mm; D XIV–XV, 10–12; A III, 8–9. 27–29 scales in the lateral line, which is in two sections. Body shape ellipsoid. Head small, with small, terminal, slightly upturned mouth. Eyes large. Pectoral fins short. Tips of dorsal and anal fins extend to beyond base of the tail fin. Tail fin rounded. Head iridescent green and blue, lower jaw blue. Body olive or iridescent green, with 8–9 olive-mauve bars. Belly off-white. Fins mauve or yellow. Soft dorsal, anal and tail fins distinctly spotted, with radial lines on the posterior dorsal fin. Pelvic fins sooty. Juveniles with black 'tilapia spot' at the base of the dorsal fin and a further spot on the gill cover. Breeding females dark greenish-black. Breeding males have a mauve head. Males larger than females.

The smallest tilapia in the Okavango Delta. An uncommon species that inhabits turbid, highly enriched floodplain lagoons in the panhandle and perennial upper swamp and floodplains, and in the shallow well-vegetated margins of channels in the seasonal lower swamp and Thamalakane and Boteti rivers. It feeds on detritus, soft plants and aquatic insect larvae. Between September and February spawning takes place in isolated floodplain lagoons, where the males establish a territory, dig shallow, saucer-shaped nests in the mud, and attract ripe females. The females deposit up to 400 eggs in the nest, where they are fertilized. The nest is defended mainly by the female, while the male guards the territory. The eggs and fry may be moved to alternative brood pits dug by the female. The eggs hatch after 3–4 days, and the fry soon become free-swimming. In isolated pools with low levels of dissolved oxygen the fry may 'hang' from the water surface and take oxygen from the air. Okavango tilapia are patchily distributed in the delta, with populations occurring in Maqwexana Pools in Moremi Game Reserve and in the Boro, Thamalakane and Boteti rivers during the high flood. Elsewhere they are found in the Kavango, upper Zambezi and southern tributaries of the Congo River. Their southern limit of distribution is the Okavango Delta. Unimportant in the subsistence fishery and too small to be of interest to anglers. An attractive aquarium species.

Banded tilapia   *Tilapia sparrmanii* A. Smith, 1840
Ditapia (B), *Izizi* (B), *Tlhapi* (S), *Pirabagana* (S)

D.P.V

TL: 240 mm; D XIII–XV, 9–11; A III, 9–10. 27–29 scales in the lateral line, which is in two sections. Deep-bodied and ovoid, with a small, terminal mouth. Eyes large. Scales cycloid. Pectoral fins short. Tips of the dorsal and anal fins extend to the end of the caudal peduncle. Colour olive-green with 8–9 vertical bars on body, some in two sections, and two bars between the eyes. Scales with brown centres. Soft rays in the dorsal and anal fins with iridescent blue spots. Belly light olive-green. Spawning pairs have a dark throat, abdomen and anal fin, with the dorsal and tail fins edged in red in males. Pectoral and anal fins light green, with green to brown spots. A prominent black 'tilapia spot' is present on the base of the dorsal fin in juveniles; it becomes less conspicuous in adults (in most other tilapias it disappears in the adults). There is also a black spot on the end of the gill cover. Lips and lower jaw light blue. Reaches 0.54 kg.

An abundant, widespread and highly adaptable small tilapia found in sheltered channels, lagoons and floodplains. Shoals in shallow, standing water with abundant plant cover. Uncommon in the open water of large lagoons. Often found together with the straightfin barb and other hardy species. Unlike many Okavango fishes it is relatively tolerant of low temperatures. Juveniles feed on small crustaceans and insect larvae, while adults eat filamentous algae, aquatic plants, plant material of terrestrial origin (leaves, berries, fruits), zooplankton, insect nymphs, worms and small fish. Predators of the banded tilapia include tigerfish, southern African pike, catfishes, largemouths, kingfishers and stalking fish-eating birds, such as storks and herons.

Banded tilapias are nest guarders, not mouthbrooders, and spawn throughout the warm months (August–April). The male makes a sand-scrape nest among plants, and attracts females with a mating dance. The eggs (up to 800 but usually 100–300) are deposited in the nest, fertilized and then aggressively guarded and continuously fanned by both parents. The eggs may also be attached to aquatic plants within the nest, or even to roots on the underside of papyrus mats. The newly hatched fry initially remain attached to plants or sand using a head gland but wriggle constantly to pass water over their gills, and may be moved by the parents from one nest to another or into a pit in the nest. Within 7–8 days they become free-swimming and feed on zooplankton, but they remain in a tight shoal that is guarded by the parents for several weeks. The adults jerk their bodies to warn the young of approaching danger.

Widely distributed in the Okavango Delta and Chobe River. Elsewhere they are distributed from the Orange River and KwaZulu-Natal south coast northwards to the southern tributaries of the Congo River, and to Lake Malawi and the Zambezi River system. Extensively stocked beyond their natural range in South Africa and Zimbabwe. They are caught in subsistence trap and net fisheries. They are of little interest to anglers because of their small size, although they may be caught on a small hook using worm bait and are frequently used as live bait to catch larger fish species. They are attractive and hardy aquarium fish. Named after the Swedish naturalist Anders Sparrman, who sailed around the world with Captain Cook and visited South Africa in the 1770s.

Small, colourful fishes known for their hardiness. Excellent aquarium pets. Dorsal and anal fins lack spines. Single dorsal fin is placed far back over the anal fin. Dorsal and anal fins are nearly symmetrical. Pelvic fins small and far forward. Pectoral fins low on the body. Egg-laying fishes, they inhabit tropical regions in Africa, Madagascar, India and southeast Asia. Previously placed in the family Aplocheilidae. One species known from the region.

Caprivi killifish   *Nothobranchius capriviensis* Watters, Wildekamp & Shidlovskiy, 2015

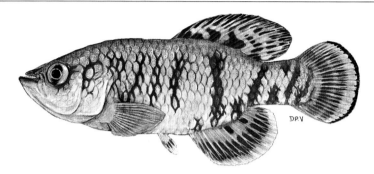

Avg L: 40–45 mm, SL: 50 mm; D 16–17; A 16–18. 27–32 scales along body. Head large, covered in scales. Eyes large and yellow, with a vertical black band. Mouth dorsal, lower jaw projecting beyond upper jaw. Body robust. Pectoral fin low on body. Dorsal fin far back, above the anal fin and about equal in size. Tail fin large and rounded. Body iridescent blue, with irregular vertical red bars. Dorsal fin heavily marked with red. Anal and tail fins with black, blue and red bands. Males grow larger than females and are more brightly coloured. **Endangered**

A small killifish that inhabits temporary pans and swamps in the upper Zambezi system and Chobe River in the Zambezi Region (formerly the Caprivi Strip), Namibia; not known from the Okavango Delta. Their preferred habitats typically have a substrate of fine, soft black mud that is rich in the clays that occur in low-lying mopane woodland. In periods of heavy rainfall and flooding it, like other killifishes, is able to move freely away from the pans in which it hatched to colonize new pans, which then become isolated when the floodwaters subside. Feeds on insects and other aquatic invertebrates. Males perform displays with their colourful fins to attract females and pair off. Spawning takes place daily for an extended period, with a few eggs laid at a time. The fish grow to maturity in a few weeks. When the habitats dry up, the adult fish die and the developing embryos within the eggs survive the dry season encased in muddy clay. Killifishes are known as annual fishes as they usually complete their life cycle within one year.

This species was first collected by Ben van der Waal from two shallow seasonal pools south of Katima Mulilo in the upper Zambezi River (in the then Caprivi Strip). It is endangered, as its only known habitat is threatened by road building and pollution.

LIVE-BEARERS AND TOPMINNOWS · Poeciliidae

Small, brightly coloured fishes that live in the water column or near the water surface. Dorsal fin far back over anal fin, and neither has any spines. Anal fin large and near-symmetrical with the dorsal fin. Pectoral fin low on body. Pelvic fins far back. Tail fin rounded. Eyes large, blue. Large scales, no lateral line. Popular aquarium fishes. The topminnows were previously placed in the family Cyprinodontidae and the genus *Aplocheilichthys*, but they are now placed in the family Poeciliidae, subfamily Procatopodinae, and the genus *Micropanchax*. Five species are known from the region.

Johnston's topminnow · *Micropanchax johnstoni* (Günther, 1893)

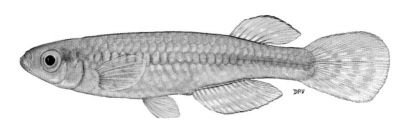

Avg L: 30 mm, TL: 60 mm; D 8–9; A 11–14. 23–25 scales in lateral series. Head small and mouth terminal and upturned, with projecting lower jaw. Eye large, silver-blue. Body slender, elongate. Dorsal fin far back, over posterior anal fin rays. Tail fin large and rounded. Iridescent blue patch on upper gill cover. Body coloration translucent yellow-green with silvery blue iridescence on body scales. Belly off-white. Males more colourful than females. Fins clear in females but light yellow with dark yellow spots in males. Thin black edge to dorsal, tail and anal fins in adults.

Probably the most widely distributed fish in the Okavango Delta. An abundant topminnow that inhabits backwaters, floodplains, swamps and vegetated lagoons with standing or slow-flowing water. Uncommon along the fringes of the mainstream channels or in strong-flowing water. Often swims in small shoals near the water surface and among weeds, where it seeks refuge and food. Feeds on small invertebrates such as mosquito larvae, midges, mayflies and daphnia. Its predators include kingfishers and cormorants. A serial spawner that lays regular batches of eggs on plants throughout the year, except in June and July. The eggs hatch after 15–20 days, and the young fish reach sexual maturity within six months. Common throughout the Okavango Delta and Chobe River. Elsewhere occurs in the Kavango and Zambezi systems, the catchments of Lake Malawi and Lake Rukwa, and in east coast rivers in Tanzania and Mozambique. It was used as an indicator species for toxicity tests during the aerial spraying control programme for tsetse fly in Botswana in the early 1990s. Named after Sir Harry Johnston, who collected the species in Lake Malawi in the 1880s for the British Museum.

Striped topminnow *Micropanchax katangae* (Boulenger, 1912)

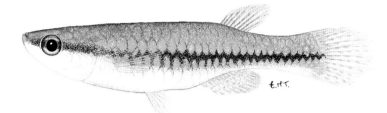

Avg L: 45 mm, SL: 55 mm; D 8–10; A 14–15. 25–28 scales in lateral series. Mouth terminal, upturned. Eyes large, yellow. Deep-bodied. Dorsal fin over anal fin. Body coloration olive-brown above, white below, with a distinct black stripe from the snout to the tail fin base; the stripe has a zigzag appearance behind the pectoral fins. Iridescent blue-turquoise band behind the black stripe on flanks and caudal peduncle. Fins clear or light yellow, with bubble markings along the bases of the dorsal and anal fins. Tail fin rounded.

Common in the northern perennial areas of the Okavango Delta and upstream into Namibia, as well as in the Chobe River in dense papyrus beds, reed beds, rootballs and other aquatic vegetation. Uncommon in slow-flowing channels, floodplains and backwater lagoons in the seasonal swamp. Feeds on insect larvae, daphnia and other small invertebrates. A serial spawner that lays its eggs in batches on plants. Elsewhere it is found in the Kavango, Cunene, Zambezi, Zambian Congo, Lufira and Luapala systems and in east coast rivers southwards to Richards Bay in KwaZulu-Natal. Used as an agent for mosquito control in Botswana.

Meshscaled topminnow *Micropanchax hutereaui* (Boulenger, 1913)

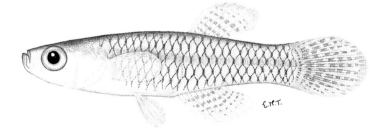

Avg L: 25–30 mm, TL: 35 mm; D 8–9; A 11–12. 23–25 scales in lateral series. Body short, deep. Mouth terminal, sharply upturned. Dorsal and anal fins symmetrical. Tail fin rounded. Colour translucent yellowish, with light iridescent blue tinges on the scales. Iris turquoise above. Sooty pigment on scale edges gives mesh effect. Bases of dorsal, anal and tail fins with dark brown square dots.

A common floodplain or marsh-living species that is also found in vegetated slower-flowing rivers and backwater lagoons. Does not migrate. Feeds on algae and aquatic insects, such as mosquito larvae. A serial spawner that lays small batches of eggs on plants throughout the breeding season. Occurs throughout the Okavango Delta and Chobe River. Elsewhere it is found in the Kavango, upper Zambezi, Zambian Congo, lower Shire and Pungwe-Buzi systems. An attractive aquarium species and potentially useful mosquito-control agent.

Pygmy topminnow *Micropanchax 'pygmy'* Undescribed new species

SL: 30 mm; D 8–9; A 11–12. 23–25 scales in lateral series. Head small, mouth terminal and upturned, with projecting lower jaw. Eye large, iris blue. Body short and deep. Dorsal fin far back, over posterior anal fin rays. Tail fin large and rounded. Colour translucent light brown with dark brown linings to scales on the upper body. Scales on mid-body turquoise. Dorsal, anal and tail fins olive-yellow with dark brown bars. Pelvic fins brown, pectoral fins clear.

The preferred habitat of this scientifically undescribed topminnow is swamps and permanent *dambos*, which are drainage channels in areas with clayey soils that cause waterlogged conditions. *Dambos* are prominent features of the Kavango and Zambezi systems. Also found in slow-flowing channels, floodplains and backwater lagoons. Feeds on insect larvae, daphnia and other small invertebrates. A serial spawner that lays its eggs in batches on plants throughout the spawning season. Found throughout the Okavango Delta and the Chobe River, as well as in the swamps and bogs of the Kavango, Kwando and upper Zambezi rivers in Namibia, Angola and Zambia.

Invasive alien fishes pose a severe threat to indigenous species in the Okavango Delta, Chobe River and confluent waterways. They not only compete with them for space and food but also carry the risk of introducing alien parasites and diseases to which the local fishes have little or no resistance. Alien fishes may also prey on indigenous species, especially their eggs and fry. Certain alien fishes also have the potential to hybridize with indigenous species, and some species have such a large impact that they disrupt entire ecological processes and change the nature of the habitat. Fortunately, no alien fishes have yet been recorded from the Okavango Delta or Chobe River (although they may be present without having been discovered), and the waters of the Okavango are too warm for many of the temperate/subtemperate aliens that have caused problems in South Africa, Zimbabwe and Namibia, such as bluegill sunfish, largemouth, smallmouth and spotted bass and, to a lesser extent, brown and rainbow trout. The following alien fishes are considered to be those that are most likely to invade the Okavango Delta and Chobe River and cause damage there.

Poeciliidae

Mosquitofish, *Gambusia affinis*

This aggressive invader originates from central and north America and was originally introduced into southern Africa for mosquito control (although we have perfectly efficient mosquito-control agents in our indigenous topminnows and other surface-feeding fishes). Alien mosquitofish are widely established in South Africa, Namibia and Zimbabwe. They threaten indigenous fish, as they prey on their larvae.

Guppy, *Poecilia reticulata*

A tropical South American species that is likely to thrive in the Okavango ecosystem and is at risk of being introduced through the aquarium trade. As Botswana has strict laws that prohibit the importation of alien species, it is unlikely that the guppy will be imported for mosquito control, as has occurred widely elsewhere.

Swordtail, *Xiphophorus helleri*
A tropical central American species
that was introduced through
the aquarium trade and
has established itself in
subtropical regions in South
Africa and in Lake Otjikoto in Namibia.
It preys on fish larvae.

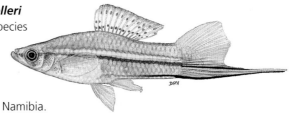

Cichlidae

Nile tilapia, *Oreochromis niloticus*
An aggressive invasive species from
central, west and north Africa that
would survive in the Okavango
Delta and Chobe River and
is highly likely to hybridize
with the threespot tilapia
and greenhead tilapia, as well
as compete with them for food and
space. It is also a potential vector of disease. It
is already established far beyond its natural range
in Zambia, Zimbabwe, Mozambique and South Africa.
The main threat of introduction is from the fish-farming industry, as hybrids of this
species grow rapidly, but Botswana has wisely banned its introduction as well as the
introduction of any other non-native species.

Israeli tilapia, *Oreochromis aureus*
A Middle Eastern and West African
species that has been introduced
into parts of South Africa
for aquaculture.

UTILIZING AND CONSERVING THE DELTA AND ITS WILDLIFE

In June 2014 the Okavango Delta was declared UNESCO's 1,000th World Heritage Site, joining Ngamiland's Tsodilo Hills as the second World Heritage Site in Botswana. This status was granted because the Okavango Delta is regarded as an extraordinary and iconic wilderness area that has been conserved for millennia by the indigenous people living in and around it, whose stewardship exemplifies the close links that should exist between nature and culture. The crystal-clear waters of the delta transform the otherwise dry Kalahari Desert into a scenic landscape of exceptional and rare beauty, and sustain an ecosystem of remarkable habitat and species diversity. The annual flood revitalizes the delta's ecosystems and is a critical life force during the peak of Botswana's dry season (June/July). The Okavango therefore displays an extraordinary juxtaposition of a vibrant wetland in an arid landscape and is an outstanding example of the complexity, interdependence and interplay of climatic, geomorphological, hydrological, and biological processes.

Factors threatening Okavango fishes

Every year hundreds of plant and animal species worldwide go extinct or become endangered because of a mix of human-caused factors, which can be summarized under five headings, forming the convenient acronym HIPPO:
- habitat destruction,
- invasive species,
- pollution,
- population growth, and
- overexploitation.

The same factors operate in the Okavango Delta and Chobe River, though to varying degrees, with habitat destruction and overexploitation (overfishing in this case) being the main areas of concern.

Habitat destruction and alteration

The main lifeblood of the Okavango and Chobe systems – the annual flow of floodwaters from the highlands in Angola – is not, at this stage, seriously impacted, but there are plans to develop the water resources of the Kavango River and its headwaters in Angola. These plans, which may include impoundments and water-diversion schemes, need to be considered carefully in terms of their long-term impact, as they could constitute a major threat to the ecology of the Okavango Delta, upon which many people, plant and animal species are dependent.

There has been some interference with water-flow patterns in the seasonal swamp and drainage rivers. The lower Boro River was canalized in the 1970s, and the spoil was piled up along the river banks. This interfered with water flow onto and off the floodplain, which will have reduced the amount of habitat available to floodplain fishes. Also, water that would have flowed towards Lake Ngami in the Nghabe River was, in the 1970s, diverted into the Boteti River so as to increase water flow to Lake Xau, the Orapa diamond mine and irrigation farms. Other forms of habitat alteration have also taken place, such as bush clearing, uncontrolled use of fires to create grazing for cattle, and the encroachment of farmland onto floodplains.

In the late 1980s the Southern Okavango Integrated Water Development Project proposed that a reservoir should be built on the Thamalakane near Maun and that 42 km of the Boro River up to Nxaragha Lagoon should be dredged to enhance water flow into the reservoir, but the Botswana Government terminated this project in 1992. The Okavango River Basin Commission (OKACOM) was established in 1994 so that sustainable levels of water utilization from the Okavango Delta could be determined holistically for the benefit of the long-term conservation of the whole ecosystem.

An important component of environmental management is not interfering with the natural functioning of systems. The 'natural ecosystem engineers' of the Okavango Delta are the hippos, elephants and termites whose activities have shaped the delta and its floodplains for millennia. Their activities must be allowed to continue, and we should also resist any temptation to stabilize the system, such as canalizing channels, draining swamps or impeding floodwater flow, as its natural condition is an 'unstable stability', with cycles of change repeating themselves year after year. The free movement of wildlife is also important to the delta ecosystem, as animal droppings fertilize newly flooded waterbodies.

Invasive species

The Okavango Delta and Chobe River have not, as yet, suffered from extensive invasions by alien fishes, although we may simply not know about recent fish invasions into these systems. As indicated in the section on 'The region's invasive aliens' (p. 109), there is, however, a danger that the delta and adjacent rivers will be invaded by Nile tilapia (Oreochromis niloticus), Israeli tilapia (Oreochromis aureus) and common carp (Cyprinus carpio), and possibly also by popular aquarium fishes, such as mosquitofish (Gambusia affinis) and guppies (Poecilia reticulata). Carp, which are hardy and adaptable, have invaded waterbodies in all adjacent countries and would probably thrive in both clear and turbid water environments in the Okavango Delta and Chobe River if they were introduced. An even greater threat is posed by the parasitic water mould Aphanomyces invadans, which causes redspot disease in indigenous fishes and has already been recorded in the Chobe and Okavango Delta and the Cubango River in Angola.

Invasive aquatic invertebrates also pose a threat to the Okavango and Chobe systems. They include the red swamp crayfish (Procambarus clarkii) from North America, which has invaded and caused havoc in waterbodies in Kenya, Uganda, Egypt, Sudan and South Africa, and three freshwater crayfishes from Australia, the Australian red claw crayfish (Cherax quadricarinatus), smooth marron (C. cainii) and yabbie (C. destructor). Fortunately the marron and yabbie have not established wild populations outside aquaculture facilities, but the Australian red claw crayfish has invaded large areas of Zambia, including the Kafue Flats and Barotseland floodplain as well as Lake Kariba, and there is a high risk that it will soon reach the Chobe and Okavango systems. Alien crayfishes alter aquatic habitats, compete with indigenous crustaceans and introduce alien parasites and diseases.

Kariba weed *(Salvinia molesta)*, an alien floating aquatic plant, has spread throughout vast areas of Africa, clogging waterways and necessitating expensive control programmes. It first invaded the Chobe River in northern Botswana over 50 years ago and the first outbreak in the Okavango Delta was reported in 1986. In the absence of natural predators, *Salvinia* spreads rapidly and excludes sunlight from waterbodies, which interferes with the ability of submerged plants to photosynthesize and produce oxygen. This, in turn, adversely affects fishes – populations are lower in *Salvinia*-infested waterbodies.

In the late 1980s the Botswana Department of Water Affairs launched a successful biological control programme on *Salvinia* using a small weevil *(Cyrtobagous salviniae)* from South America. This weevil feeds only on *Salvinia* and does not threaten any indigenous plants or animals. Control should be exercised over gill nets being brought into Botswana from neighbouring countries, as they are known to spread *Salvinia*.

Pollution

The Okavango Delta and Chobe River have fortunately not suffered from major pollution problems, although the early use of DDT, and later aerial spraying of Endosulfan, to control tsetse flies, did cause mortalities among aquatic insects and fishes. In 1991 a team from the JLB Smith Institute of Ichthyology (now SAIAB), including the authors of this book, recommended that Deltamethrin should be sprayed instead of Endosulfan, as the former was demonstrated to be less harmful to aquatic life and other non-target species. Insecticide spraying is no longer carried out over the Okavango Delta but land-based use of insecticides may still cause localized pollution.

Water pollution may also be caused by artificial fertilizers that are used on adjacent farmland, or sprayed insecticides that are used in domestic settings, which wash into natural waterways, as occurs throughout Africa. The use of insecticide-impregnated mosquito nets as fishing nets also poses a threat, as the insecticide may dissolve in the water and accumulate up the food chain. Fortunately, Roussel, the manufacturers of Deltamethrin, have now developed mosquito nets impregnated with Deltamethrin, which is not water soluble.

Population growth

Human population growth in Botswana, and in the Ngamiland District, is a developing problem, not only because of fishing pressure but also because of the local overutilization of some wetland resources, such as reeds for hut-making.

Overexploitation (overfishing)

Fisheries research by different organizations since the 1980s has revealed that local artisanal fishermen harvest aquatic resources in the Okavango Delta on a sustainable basis either by traditional fishing methods or by means of small-scale commercial operations using gill nets. In contrast, overfishing by foreign commercial and semi-commercial fishermen is a major concern. Until recently, most of their fishing effort was focused on Lake Ngami, where the number of fishermen increased from about 200 in 2011 to over 3,000 in 2014. This greatly increased fishing effort deprived local fishermen of their catch and led to large quantities of dried fish being exported from Botswana each year.

It could be argued that the fishes of Lake Ngami are doomed anyway during the drying-up cycle, but it still makes sense for local people (and animals) to be the main beneficiaries of this resource. Fisheries management plans need to be dynamic and take into account the ebb and flow of ecosystems like Lake Ngami when determining sustainable harvesting rates that depend on prevailing hydrological conditions. The longer-term danger is that, if Lake Ngami is dry over several annual cycles, foreign fishermen will turn their attention to the fish stocks of the delta itself, where they will come into direct conflict with the traditional fishermen who have harvested this resource for centuries. However, if Lake Ngami remains full over several wet cycles, it would provide a valuable source of protein for local people.

Prior to the recent introduction of legislation banning commercial fishing in the delta, tour operators in the riverine panhandle and the seasonal swamp reported increasing numbers of illegal gill nets being laid there, which would constitute a serious threat to Okavango fishes. In the riverine panhandle Hambukushu fishermen from the Zambezi Region of Namibia have fished with gill nets for decades and this activity has been accepted by the local authorities. On the Chobe River illegal gill nets are regularly set on the Namibian side of the river near Kasane.

The problem is that the scale and impact of these illegal fisheries, which use highly efficient modern gear, are largely unknown and it is therefore difficult, if not impossible, to develop and implement effective management policies and practices that will reduce their impact and maintain essential ecological processes in the delta. Sustained fishing using modern monofilament gill nets, as well as seine nets and throw nets, has already devastated the fish stocks of other wetlands in the upper Zambezi system and those associated with the African Great Lakes and the major rivers of central Africa.

Fortunately Botswana's authorities have reacted quickly to the threat and it is now illegal to export dried or salted fishes from the Okavango Delta or lakes Ngami or Xau to any country. It is also illegal to carry out any commercial fishing in the Okavango Delta north of the 'Buffalo Fence'. Stiff penalties, including fines and prison sentences, have been introduced for any transgressors of the law. These are positive and effective management steps and should reduce or even eliminate the risk of illegal fishing in the delta.

Most recently, in 2017, Botswana's Ministry of Environment, Natural Resources Conservation and Tourism (MENT) implemented a management strategy that ensures that Batswana fishermen are able to participate fully in, and benefit the most from, the fishing industry in the Okavango Delta and other waterbodies in the country. Efforts are also being made to develop the freshwater fish market in Botswana. Furthermore, the ban on fishing in lakes Ngami and Xau was lifted in December 2016, and fishing permits and licences have once again been issued in the different areas to allow people to fish. The ministry has also made it clear that the export of fresh fish from Botswana is allowed and is ongoing, and that the only prohibition that is in place is with regard to the export of dried fish. The government has undertaken to continue to consult and engage with different stakeholders on the development and regulation of the fishing industry in Botswana for the benefit of locals.

GLOSSARY OF TECHNICAL TERMS

Adipose fin: Fleshy fin without rays behind the rayed dorsal fin.

Adult: Sexually mature life stage capable of breeding.

Aestivate: Exist in a dormant state during a hot, dry period.

Alien: Species that does not naturally occur in an area but has been introduced.

Anal fin: Ventral fin in the midline behind the anus.

Anterior: Near or towards the front.

Average length (AL): Average length of a large sample of fish.

Barbel: Fleshy filament (feeler) growing from around the mouth or snout of a fish, used as an organ of taste and touch.

Benthic: On or near the bottom.

Branched ray: Divided, segmented fin ray.

Branchial: Related to the gills.

Brood size: Number of young that hatch or are born at a single breeding event.

Caudal fin: Tail fin.

Caudal peduncle: Section of a fish's body from the anal fin to the base of the tail fin.

Cichlid: Member of the family Cichlidae, including breams, largemouths, tilapiines and haplochromines.

Compressed: Flattened from side to side.

Ctenoid: Scale with small tooth-like projections along the outer edge.

Cycloid: Scale with a smooth outer edge.

Dambo: Drainage line in an area of impeded flow due to clayey soils, resulting in waterlogging and thus the exclusion of trees.

Depressed: Flattened from top to bottom.

Detritus: Dead particulate organic matter that settles on the substrate and is typically colonized by micro-organisms that decompose it.

Diurnal: During daylight hours.

Dorsal: Uppermost surface.

Dorsal fin: Fin in the midline on the upper part of a fish's body.

Egg-spot: Spot (or spots) on the anal fin that resembles an egg, found in many cichlids.

Electric organ: Specialized organ in some fishes, such as snoutfishes, used for generating electricity, either to communicate, detect prey or deter predators.

Electrogenic: Able to generate electricity.

Electroreception: Ability of a fish, such as catfishes, to detect natural electrical stimuli.

Emarginate: Having an indented or notched margin on the tail fin.

Embryo: Very early life stage of a fish that develops from the fertilized egg and is still dependent on the egg yolk for food.

Endemic: Native to and occurring naturally in a place.

Filamentous: Thin and thread-like.

Finning: Habit of some cichlids, especially three-spot bream, that swim at the water surface, flapping their fins out of the water, while sucking in oxygen-rich surface water.

Floodplain: Area of low-lying ground adjacent to a river, formed mainly of river sediments and subject to flooding.

Fork length (FL): Length of a fish from snout tip to the tip of the rays in the middle of the tail fin.

Fry: Informal term for young fishes, which may include the embryo, larva and juvenile stages.

Fusiform: Widest in the middle and tapered at both ends.

Gill arch: Slender, bony arch in the throat of a fish that supports the gill filaments. There are normally four or five pairs of gill arches.

Gill cover (opercle): Bony, hinged cover over the gill chamber on both sides of the head of a fish.

Gill filaments: Thread-like structures in the gills of fishes that have a large surface area and form the respiratory surface for extracting oxygen from the water.

Gill rakers: Projections along the front edge of the gill arches that sieve the water passing between the gill arches and prevent food from being washed out.

Gonads: Internal reproductive organs (female ovaries and male testes).

Gravid: Carrying ripe eggs.

Habitat: Place where a fish lives.

Humeral process: Bony process sticking out backwards from the pectoral girdle above the pectoral fin. Conspicuous in squeakers.

Ichthyology: Scientific study of fishes.

Inferior: Below or underneath, opposite of superior.

Invasive species: Species that are not native to an area but have been introduced (intentionally or accidentally) and may adversely affect the habitats and communities that they invade economically, environmentally and/or ecologically.

Juvenile: Life stage of a fish between an embryo or larva and an adult.

Larva: Life stage of a fish between the embryo and juvenile in those species that include this feeding stage in their development.

Lateral line scale count: Number of pored scales on the lateral line on either side of the body.

Lateral series: Number of scale rows along the length of the body of a fish without a lateral line.

Live-bearer: Fish that gives birth to live young (juveniles) that look like their parents.

Lunate: Shaped like a crescent moon.

Madiba: Lagoon or small, permanent lake.

Mandibular: Refers to the lower jaw, e.g. mandibular barbels.

Maxilla: Main bone of the upper jaw.

Median: In the midline.

Mulapo: Drainage line in a floodplain.

Nare: Nostril opening.

Nuptial: Related to breeding.

Omnivorous: Feeding on a wide variety of foods including plants, micro-organisms and animals.

Opercle: Gill cover.

Origin of fin: Position of the front end of the base of a fin.

Oshana: Small channels leading from a river through its floodplain.

Ovary: Female reproductive gland.

Oviduct: Tube through which eggs pass from the ovary to the genital pore in fishes.

Oviparous: Egg laying.

Pan: Seasonal, temporary waterbody without an outlet that is left behind in depressions when the floodwaters recede, or rain-filled pools in poorly drained clayey soils.

Panhandle: Channel of the Okavango River before it enters the Okavango Delta, between Shakawe and Seronga.

Papyrus: Wetland sedge.

Pectoral fin: Paired fins located behind the head.

Pelagic: Living in midwater.

Pelvic fin: Paired fins located on the ventral side of the body below or behind the pectoral fins and in front of the anal fin.

Perennial: Permanently flooded.

Piscivorous: Feeding mainly on fishes.

Plankton: Diverse group of very small plants (phytoplankton) and animals (zooplankton) that float or drift in the water column and cannot swim against a current. They are an important food source for fishes.

Posterior: Behind or near the rear end.

Ray: Strut-like supports found in the fins of most fishes.

Redspot disease: Epizootic ulcerative syndrome (EUS), a disease of fishes caused by a fungus that has invaded the Okavango Delta

Rheophilic: Preferring fast-flowing water.

Riffle: Shallow, rocky river reach with turbulent flowing water.

Sawgrass: A tall sedge, *Cladium jamaicense*, not a grass, that thrives in floodplains and on floating mats in wetlands throughout the tropics.

Scientific name: Official name of a species consisting of the genus name and the species name, always written in italics or underlined, e.g. *Hydrocynus vittatus*. Each species has only one valid scientific name.

Serrated: Saw-like

Sexual dimorphism: Differences in the form and colour of male and female fishes.

Spawning: Breeding in fishes.

Species: Group of closely related plants or animals whose members have a common history, share features that are unique to the group, and normally interbreed in nature.

Spine: Pointed bony fin support, either smooth or serrated.

Standard length (SL): Length of a fish measured in a straight line from the tip of the snout to the base of the tail fin (as indicated by the line of bending of the tail fin).

Subspecies: Taxonomic category below a species, usually a geographically isolated race.

Substrate: Surface on which a fish lives or feeds.

Sub-truncate: Almost truncate; not quite square cut.

Swim bladder: Thin-walled, gas- or fat-filled bladder in the body cavity of fishes that is used to regulate buoyancy or produce sounds.

Tail fin: Caudal fin.

Testis: Male reproductive gland.

Total length (TL): Overall length of a fish measured in a straight line from the tip of the snout to the furthest tip of the tail in its natural position.

Truncate: With a straight edge; square cut.

Tubercle: Small, horny projection on the head, fins or body.

Unbranched ray: Simple, usually flexible, segmented fin ray.

Valve trap (uMono): Traditional African fish trap made from sticks or reeds with an entrance of overlapping sticks that fish can enter but cannot easily exit.

Ventral: The lowermost surface.

Viviparous: Giving birth to live young that resemble the adults.

Yolk sac: Sac attached to an embryo that provides food in the form of egg yolk to the growing fish.

REFERENCES AND FURTHER READING

Allanson, B.R., R.C. Hart, J.H. O'Keeffe & R.D. Robarts. 1990. *Inland Waters of Southern Africa: An Ecological Perspective*. Kluwer Academic Publishers, Dordrecht. 458 pages.

Barnard, K.H. 1948. Report on a Collection of Fishes from the Okavango River, with notes on Zambezi fishes. *Annals of the South African Museum* 36: 407–458.

Bell-Cross, G. & J.L. Minshull. 1988. The Fishes of Zimbabwe. National Museums & Monuments of Zimbabwe, Harare. 294 pages.

Bills, R. 1996. Fish stock assessment of the Okavango River (May 1996). *Investigational Report of the JLB Smith Institute of Ichthyology* 56: 1–104.

Boulenger, G.A. 1911. On a collection of fishes from the Lake Ngami Basin, Bechuanaland. *Transactions of the Zoological Society of London* 18(5): 399-438.

Bruton, M.N. (ed.) 1980. Report on the 1980 Rhodes University expedition to Lake Ngami, Botswana. *Investigational Report of the JLB Smith Institute of Ichthyology* 1: 1–37.

Bruton, M.N. 2015. *When I was a Fish. Tales of an Ichthyologist*. Jacana Media, Cape Town. 315 pages.

Bruton, M.N. 2016. *Traditional Fishing Methods of Africa*. Cambridge University Press, Cape Town. 96 pages.

Bruton, M.N. & P.B.N. Jackson. 1983. Fish and fisheries of wetlands. *Journal of the Limnological Society of Southern Africa* 9(2): 123–133.

Butchart, D. 2016. *Wildlife of the Okavango* Struik Nature, Cape Town. 144 pages.

Campbell, A.C. 1976. *Proceedings of the Symposium on the Okavango Delta and its Future Utilisation*. Botswana Society, Gaborone. 350 pages.

Jackson, P.B.N. 1961. *The Fishes of Northern Rhodesia. A Checklist of Indigenous Species*. Government Printer, Lusaka. 140 pages.

Johnson, P. A. Bannister. 1977. *Okavango. Sea of Land. Land of Water*. Struik, Cape Town. 191 pages.

Jubb, R.A. 1961. *An Illustrated Guide to the Freshwater Fishes of the Zambezi River, Lake Kariba, Pungwe, Sabi, Lundi, and Limpopo Rivers*. Stuart Manning, Bulawayo. 171 pages.

Jubb, R.A. 1967. *Freshwater Fishes of Southern Africa*. A.A. Balkema, Cape Town. 248 pages.

Jubb, R.A. & I.G. Gaigher. 1971. Checklist of the fishes of Botswana. *Arnoldia Rhodesiana* 5: 1–22.

Lévêque, C., M.N. Bruton & G.W Sentongo (eds.). 1988. *Biology and Ecology of African Freshwater Fishes*. ORSTOM, Paris. 508 pages.

Marshall, B. 2011. The fishes of Zimbabwe and their biology. *Smithiana Monograph* 3: 1–290.

Merron, G.S. & M.N. Bruton. 1984. Report on the October–November 1983 expedition to the Okavango Delta, Botswana. *Investigational Report of the J.L.B. Smith Institute of Ichthyology* 8: 1–21.

Merron, G.S., M.N. Bruton & P.H. Skelton. 1984. Report on the March–April 1984 Okavango expedition. *Investigational Report of the J.L.B. Smith Institute of Ichthyology* 10: 1–27.

Merron, G.S. & M.N. Bruton. 1988. The ecology and management of the fishes of the Okavango Delta, Botswana, with special reference to the role of the seasonal floods. *Investigational Report of the J.L.B. Smith Institute of Ichthyology* 29: 1–291.

Ross, K. 2010. *Okavango. Jewel of the Kalahari*. Struik Nature, Cape Town. 216 pages.

Scudder, T., R.E. Manley, R.W. Cole, R.K. Davis, J. Green, G.W. Howard, S.W. Lawry, D. Martz, P.P. Rogers, A.R.D Taylor, S.D. Turner, G.F. White & E.P. Wright. 1993. *The IUCN Review of the South Okavango Integrated Water Development Project*. IUCN, Gland. 544 pages.

Skelton, P.H. 2001. *A Complete Guide to the Freshwater Fishes of Southern Africa*. Struik, Cape Town. 388 pages.

Skelton, P. H. 2016. Name changes and additions to the southern African freshwater fish fauna. *African Journal of Aquatic Science* 2016: 1–17.

Skelton, P.H., C.H. Hocutt, M.N. Bruton & G.S. Merron. 1983. Report on the December 1982 expedition to Lake Ngami, Botswana. *Ichthyological Bulletin of the J.L.B. Smith Institute of Ichthyology* 5: 1–6.

Skelton, P.H., M.N. Bruton, G.S. Merron & B.C.W. van der Waal. 1985. The fishes of the Okavango drainage system in Angola, South West Africa and Botswana: taxonomy and distribution. *Ichthyological Bulletin of the J.L.B. Smith Institute of Ichthyology* 50: 1–21.

Van der Waal, B.C.W. & P.H. Skelton. 1984. Checklist of the fishes of Caprivi. *Madoqua* 13(4): 303–321.

FISHES OF THE OKAVANGO DELTA AND CHOBE RIVER

SNOUTFISHES: MORMYRIDAE (PP. 32–39)
Cyphomyrus cubangoensis (Pellegrin, 1936)
Hippopotamyrus ansorgii (Boulenger, 1905)
Hippopotamyrus szaboi Kramer, Van Der Bank & Wink, 2004
Marcusenius altisambesi Kramer, Skelton, Van der Bank & Wink, 2007
Mormyrus lacerda Castelnau, 1861
Petrocephalus longicapitis Kramer, Bills, Skelton & Wink, 2012
Petrocephalus magnitrunci Kramer, Bills, Skelton & Wink, 2012
Petrocephalus okavangoensis Kramer, Bills, Skelton & Wink, 2012
Pollimyrus castelnaui (Boulenger, 1911)
Pollimyrus cuandoensis Kramer, Van der Bank & Wink, 2013
Pollimyrus marianne Kramer, Van der Bank, Flint, Sauer-Gürth & Wink, 2003

BARBS, MINNOWS, YELLOWFISHES AND LABEOS: CYPRINIDAE (PP.39–55)
Labeo cylindricus Peters, 1852
Labeo lunatus Jubb, 1963
Labeobarbus codringtonii (Boulenger, 1908)
Coptostomabarbus wittei David & Poll, 1937
Enteromius afrovernayi (Nichols & Boulton, 1927)
Enteromius barnardi (Jubb, 1965)
Enteromius barotseensis (Pellegrin, 1920)
Enteromius bifrenatus (Fowler, 1935)
Enteromius brevidorsalis (Boulenger, 1915)
Enteromius eutaenia (Boulenger, 1904)
Enteromius fasciolatus (Günther, 1868)
Enteromius haasianus (David, 1936)
Enteromius kerstenii (Peters, 1868)
Enteromius lineomaculatus (Boulenger, 1903)
Enteromius multilineatus (Worthington, 1933)
Enteromius paludinosus (Peters, 1852)
Enteromius poechii (Steindachner, 1911)
Enteromius radiatus (Peters, 1853)
Enteromius thamalakanensis (Fowler, 1935)
Enteromius unitaeniatus (Günther, 1866)
Opsaridium zambezense (Peters, 1852)

CITHARINES: DISTICHODONTIDAE (PP. 55-57)
Nannocharax machadoi (Poll, 1967)
Nannocharax macropterus Pellegrin, 1926
Nannocharax multifasciatus (Boulenger, 1923)

ROBBERS AND TIGERFISH: ALESTIDAE (PP. 57–61)
Brycinus lateralis (Boulenger, 1900)
Hydrocynus vittatus Castelnau, 1861
Micralestes acutidens (Peters, 1852)
Rhabdalestes maunensis (Fowler, 1935)

AFRICAN PIKES: HEPSETIDAE (PP. 62–63)
Hepsetus cuvieri (Castelnau, 1861)

MOUNTAIN CATFISH AND SAND CATLETS: AMPHILIIDAE (PP. 64–66)
Amphilius uranoscopus (Pfeffer, 1889)
Zaireichthys conspicuus Eccles, Tweddle & Skelton, 2011
Zaireichthys kavangoensis Eccles, Tweddle & Skelton, 2011
Zaireichthys pallidus Eccles, Tweddle & Skelton, 2011

AIR-BREATHING CATFISHES: CLARIIDAE (PP. 67–73)
Clarias gariepinus (Burchell, 1822)
Clarias ngamensis Castelnau, 1861
Clarias stappersii Boulenger, 1915
Clarias liocephalus Boulenger, 1898
Clarias theodorae Weber, 1897
Clariallabes platyprosopos Jubb, 1964

CLAROTEID CATFISHES: CLAROTEIDAE (PP. 73–74)
Parauchenoglanis ngamensis (Boulenger, 1911)

SQUEAKERS AND SUCKERMOUTHS: MOCHOKIDAE (PP. 74–80)
Chiloglanis fasciatus Pellegrin, 1936
Synodontis nigromaculatus Boulenger, 1905
Synodontis woosnami Boulenger, 1911
Synodontis macrostigma Boulenger, 1911
Synodontis macrostoma Skelton & White, **1990**
Synodontis leopardinus Pellegrin, 1914
Synodontis thamalakanensis Fowler, 1935
Synodontis vanderwaali Skelton & White, 1990

BUTTER CATFISHES: SCHILBEIDAE (PP. 81–82)
Schilbe intermedius Rüppell, 1832

SPINY EELS: MASTACEMBELIDAE (PP. 82–83)
Mastacembelus frenatus Boulenger, 1901
Mastacembelus vanderwaali Skelton, 1976

LABYRINTH FISHES: ANABANTIDAE (PP. 84–85)
Microctenopoma intermedium (Pellegrin, 1920)
Ctenopoma multispine Peters, 1844

RIVER BREAMS, SARGOS, LARGEMOUTH BREAMS, HAPLOCHROMINES AND TILAPIINES: CICHLIDAE (PP. 96–104)
Coptodon rendalli (Boulenger, 1897)
Hemichromis elongatus (Guichenot, 1861)
Oreochromis andersonii (Castelnau, 1861)
Oreochromis macrochir (Boulenger, 1912)
Pharyngochromis acuticeps (Steindachner, 1866)
Pseudocrenilabrus philander (Weber, 1897)
Sargochromis carlottae (Boulenger, 1905)
Sargochromis codringtonii (Boulenger, 1908)
Sargochromis giardi (Pellegrin, 1903)
Sargochromis greenwoodi (Bell-Cross, 1975)
Serranochromis altus Winemiller & Kelso-Winemiller, 1991
Serranochromis angusticeps (Boulenger, 1907)
Serranochromis longimanus (Boulenger, 1911)
Serranochromis macrocephalus (Boulenger, 1899)
Serranochromis robustus (Günther, 1864)
Serranochromis thumbergi (Castelnau, 1861)
Tilapia ruweti (Poll & Thys van den Audenaerde, 1965)
Tilapia sparrmanii A. Smith, 1840

ANNUAL KILLIFISHES: NOTHOBRANCHIDAE (P. 105)
Nothobranchius capriviensis Watters, Wildekamp & Shidlovskiy, 2015

LIVE-BEARERS AND TOPMINNOWS: POECILIIDAE (PP. 106–108)
Micropanchax johnstoni (Günther, 1893)
Micropanchax katangae (Boulenger, 1912)
Micropanchax hutereaui (Boulenger, 1913)
Micropanchax 'pygmy' Undescribed new species

INDEX TO SCIENTIFIC AND COMMON NAMES